The *Brave* Guide

From Surviving To Thriving

Personal Guide & Workbook

For Surviving Addiction And Thriving In Sobriety

The Brave Guide: From Surviving To Thriving by Diana Lea

Copyright © 2023 by DIANA LEA
Published by IMAGINATE PUBLISHING.

All rights reserved under the United States, Pan-American and International Copyright Convention.

No part of this publication may be stored in any retrieval system, reproduced, distributed, or transmitted in any form, either in whole or in part, or by any means, including photocopying, recording, or other electronic or mechanical methods, without the prior written permission from Imaginate Publishing, except in the case of brief quotations embodied in critical reviews and certain other noncommercial uses permitted by copyright law. For permissions contact: www.imiganiteonline.com

Printed in the United States

First Printing, 2023

First Edition 2023

ISBN-13: 9798387597589

Imaginate Publishing
Florida, United States

Disclaimer: The information contained in this book is for informational and educational purposes only and should not be used as a substitute for professional medical advice, diagnosis, or treatment. If you have a medical issue, it is recommended that you consult with your physician or other qualified healthcare provider.

Disclaimer: Every reasonable effort has been made to ensure that the information provided in this book was correct at the time of publication. The author and publisher do not assume and hereby disclaim any responsibility and/or liability for any loss, damage, disruption, or adverse effects resulting from the use and application, whether directly or indirectly, of the information presented within this book, whether by errors, omissions, negligence, accident, or any other cause.

Books published by Imaginate Publishing are available at special discount rates for bulk purchases by corporations, institutions, and other organizations. For more information, please contact Imaginate Publishing at www.imaginateonline.com

From the Author

I want you to know that, since you dared to picked up this book and consider sobriety, *you* are bold, *you* are brave, *you* are strong, and *you* are capable of overcoming any obstacle that comes your way.

It is my sincere hope that this book can help guide you toward a new found peace and a realization of your dream for a fulfilling life of sobriety.

Sincerely,

Diana Lea

April 3, 2023

Contents

INTRODUCTION TO THE BRAVE GUIDE	1
DAILY CHECK-IN & JOURNAL	2
THE IMPERATIVE OF SELF-CARE	31
MINDFULNESS PRACTICES	46
IDENTIFYING AND MANAGING TRIGGERS	64
UNDERSTANDING ACCEPTANCE AND SURRENDER	78
FORGIVENESS AND MAKING AMENDS	99
SUMMARY & RESOURCES:	116
TRIGGER TRACKER	122
MORE FROM IMAGINATE PUBLISHING	132

Introduction to the Brave Guide

Welcome to The Bold & Brave's *The Brave Guide*. This supplemental guide is designed to provide additional support and guidance to those of us that are working a 12-step or any other addiction recovery program. *The Brave Guide* is an excellent complement to The Bold & Brave's *AA Powerful 12 Step Workbook*, but can also be used as a standalone resource for those of us seeking additional support during our recovery journey.

Recovery from addiction can be a challenging and, at times, very overwhelming journey. It's common to experience feelings of anxiety, fear, and uncertainty about the future amongst other things. However, with the right tools and resources, it is possible to overcome addiction and live a happy and fulfilling life of sobriety. *FREEDOM!*

The Brave Guide is designed to help us gain a deeper understanding of our addiction. It provides practical tools and exercises that can help us manage our cravings and triggers, maintain our sobriety in the long term, and build a stronger sense of connection and purpose in our lives.

Throughout *The Brave Guide*, we will find a variety of tools, such as personal reflection exercises, mindfulness practices, ideas for managing triggers, and tips for self-care. These tools are designed to support our recovery journey and help us develop a deeper sense of self-awareness and understanding.

The Bold & Brave sincerely hopes that *The Brave Guide* will be a valuable resource as we navigate the challenges and opportunities of a 12-step or other addiction recovery program. The Bold & Brave encourages us to use it as a tool for personal growth and healing and to share it with others who may benefit from its resources.

Let us embark on this journey together with courage, compassion, and a willingness to learn and grow.

Daily Check-in & Journal

Keeping a daily journal and check-in is a great idea, especially for those of us in addiction recovery. It can help us to reflect on our progress and feelings throughout our recovery journey. It can also serve as a way to track our self-care practices and identify any areas we may need to improve on.

It's also a great way to provide us with a structured and consistent way to reflect on our progress and experiences throughout the recovery process.

Having a daily journal and check-in can be a very helpful tool in maintaining accountability and consistency in self-care practices. It can also help to track progress and identify areas for improvement over time. Additionally, the act of daily journaling can be therapeutic and provide a space for reflection and self-expression. And it helps us to hold ourselves accountable without even realizing that we are doing it

A person can really get to know and accept themselves better which in turn can help them to cultivate true self-love. Self-love and self-acceptance are crucial components of addiction recovery, and journaling can be a powerful tool for fostering those qualities.

When we take the time to reflect on our thoughts, feelings, and behaviors, we gain a deeper understanding of ourselves and can develop greater compassion and empathy for ourselves. We can also identify patterns or habits that are not serving us and work to change them. Overall, journaling is an excellent way to cultivate self-awareness and self-love, and is the reason I am including it in this workbook.

Date: _____ / _____ / _____ | **DAYS SOBER** | MOOD RATING: ☆☆☆☆☆

DAILY QUOTE: *I am capable of surrendering addiction to win sobriety*

Something nice I said to (*insert name*):

How I feel about yesterday's progress:

A setback or struggle I had:

A win I had:

A fear or concern I have:

One positive thing that happened today:

What I learned today:

TODAY'S ACTION LIST
Morning Prayer/Meditation ☐
Read Scripture/Recovery Lit ☐
Attended a Meeting ☐
Called Someone Sober ☐
Showered ☐ Teeth Brushed ☐
Water I Drank   1 2 3 4 5 6 7 8
Hours I Slept   1 2 3 4 5 6 7 8

TODAY I'M GRATEFUL FOR
1. _____
2. _____
3. _____

TODAY'S AGENDA	TIME

3 SELF-CARE THINGS I DID

MY RELATIONSHIPS CORNER

Date: _____ / _____ / _____ | **DAYS SOBER** | MOOD RATING: ☆☆☆☆☆

DAILY QUOTE: *I choose to focus on progress, not perfection*

- Something nice I said to (*insert name*):

- How I feel about yesterday's progress:

- A setback or struggle I had:

- A win I had:

- A fear or concern I have:

- One positive thing that happened today:

- What I learned today:

TODAY'S ACTION LIST
Morning Prayer/Meditation ☐
Read Scripture/Recovery Lit ☐
Attended a Meeting ☐
Called Someone Sober ☐
Showered ☐   Teeth Brushed ☐
Water I Drank   1 2 3 4 5 6 7 8
Hours I Slept   1 2 3 4 5 6 7 8

TODAY I'M GRATEFUL FOR
1. _____
2. _____
3. _____

TODAY'S AGENDA	TIME

3 SELF-CARE THINGS I DID

MY RELATIONSHIPS CORNER

Date: _____ / _____ / _____   **DAYS SOBER** [____]   MOOD RATING: ☆☆☆☆☆

DAILY QUOTE: *I am stronger than my addiction*

Something nice I said to (*insert name*):

How I feel about yesterday's progress:

A setback or struggle I had:

A win I had:

A fear or concern I have:

One positive thing that happened today:

What I learned today:

TODAY'S ACTION LIST
Morning Prayer/Meditation ☐
Read Scripture/Recovery Lit ☐
Attended a Meeting ☐
Called Someone Sober ☐
Showered ☐   Teeth Brushed ☐
Water I Drank   1 2 3 4 5 6 7 8
Hours I Slept   1 2 3 4 5 6 7 8

TODAY I'M GRATEFUL FOR
1. _____
2. _____
3. _____

TODAY'S AGENDA	TIME

3 SELF-CARE THINGS I DID

MY RELATIONSHIPS CORNER

Date: _____ / _____ / _____ | **DAYS SOBER** | MOOD RATING: ☆☆☆☆☆

DAILY QUOTE: *Each day is a new opportunity*

- Something nice I said to (*insert name*):

- How I feel about yesterday's progress:

- A setback or struggle I had:

- A win I had:

- A fear or concern I have:

- One positive thing that happened today:

- What I learned today:

TODAY'S ACTION LIST
Morning Prayer/Meditation ☐
Read Scripture/Recovery Lit ☐
Attended a Meeting ☐
Called Someone Sober ☐
Showered ☐ Teeth Brushed ☐
Water I Drank 1 2 3 4 5 6 7 8
Hours I Slept 1 2 3 4 5 6 7 8

TODAY I'M GRATEFUL FOR
1. _____
2. _____
3. _____

TODAY'S AGENDA	TIME

3 SELF-CARE THINGS I DID

MY RELATIONSHIPS CORNER

Date: _____ / _____ / _____ | **DAYS SOBER** | MOOD RATING: ☆☆☆☆☆

DAILY QUOTE: *I am capable of overcoming any obstacle*

Something nice I said to (*insert name*):

How I feel about yesterday's progress:

A setback or struggle I had:

A win I had:

A fear or concern I have:

One positive thing that happened today:

What I learned today:

TODAY'S ACTION LIST
Morning Prayer/Meditation ☐
Read Scripture/Recovery Lit ☐
Attended a Meeting ☐
Called Someone Sober ☐
Showered ☐ Teeth Brushed ☐
Water I Drank 1 2 3 4 5 6 7 8
Hours I Slept   1 2 3 4 5 6 7 8

TODAY I'M GRATEFUL FOR
1. _____
2. _____
3. _____

TODAY'S AGENDA	TIME

3 SELF-CARE THINGS I DID

MY RELATIONSHIPS CORNER

Date: _____ / _____ / _____ | **DAYS SOBER** | MOOD RATING: ☆☆☆☆☆

DAILY QUOTE: *I am worthy of love*

- Something nice I said to (*insert name*):

- How I feel about yesterday's progress:

- A setback or struggle I had:

- A win I had:

- A fear or concern I have:

- One positive thing that happened today:

- What I learned today:

TODAY'S ACTION LIST
Morning Prayer/Meditation ☐
Read Scripture/Recovery Lit ☐
Attended a Meeting ☐
Called Someone Sober ☐
Showered ☐ Teeth Brushed ☐
Water I Drank   1 2 3 4 5 6 7 8
Hours I Slept   1 2 3 4 5 6 7 8

TODAY I'M GRATEFUL FOR
1. _____
2. _____
3. _____

TODAY'S AGENDA	TIME

3 SELF-CARE THINGS I DID

MY RELATIONSHIPS CORNER

Date: _____ / _____ / _____ **DAYS SOBER** ☐ MOOD RATING: ☆☆☆☆☆

DAILY QUOTE: *I am grateful for the progress I have made*

Something nice I said to (*insert name*):

How I feel about yesterday's progress:

A setback or struggle I had:

A win I had:

A fear or concern I have:

One positive thing that happened today:

What I learned today:

TODAY'S ACTION LIST
Morning Prayer/Meditation ☐
Read Scripture/Recovery Lit ☐
Attended a Meeting ☐
Called Someone Sober ☐
Showered ☐ Teeth Brushed ☐
Water I Drank 1 2 3 4 5 6 7 8
Hours I Slept 1 2 3 4 5 6 7 8

TODAY I'M GRATEFUL FOR
1. _____
2. _____
3. _____

TODAY'S AGENDA	TIME

3 SELF-CARE THINGS I DID

MY RELATIONSHIPS CORNER

Date: _____ / _____ / _____ | **DAYS SOBER** | MOOD RATING: ☆☆☆☆☆

DAILY QUOTE: *My mistakes do not define me*

- Something nice I said to (*insert name*):

- How I feel about yesterday's progress:

- A setback or struggle I had:

- A win I had:

- A fear or concern I have:

- One positive thing that happened today:

- What I learned today:

TODAY'S ACTION LIST
Morning Prayer/Meditation ☐
Read Scripture/Recovery Lit ☐
Attended a Meeting ☐
Called Someone Sober ☐
Showered ☐   Teeth Brushed ☐
Water I Drank   1 2 3 4 5 6 7 8
Hours I Slept   1 2 3 4 5 6 7 8

TODAY I'M GRATEFUL FOR
1. _____
2. _____
3. _____

TODAY'S AGENDA	TIME

3 SELF-CARE THINGS I DID

MY RELATIONSHIPS CORNER

Date: _____ / _____ / _____ | **DAYS SOBER** | MOOD RATING: ☆☆☆☆☆

DAILY QUOTE: *I am constantly learning and growing*

- Something nice I said to (*insert name*):

- How I feel about yesterday's progress:

- A setback or struggle I had:

- A win I had:

- A fear or concern I have:

- One positive thing that happened today:

- What I learned today:

TODAY'S ACTION LIST
Morning Prayer/Meditation ☐
Read Scripture/Recovery Lit ☐
Attended a Meeting ☐
Called Someone Sober ☐
Showered ☐   Teeth Brushed ☐
Water I Drank   1 2 3 4 5 6 7 8
Hours I Slept   1 2 3 4 5 6 7 8

TODAY I'M GRATEFUL FOR
1. _____
2. _____
3. _____

TODAY'S AGENDA	TIME

3 SELF-CARE THINGS I DID

MY RELATIONSHIPS CORNER

Date: _____ / _____ / _____ | **DAYS SOBER** | MOOD RATING: ☆☆☆☆☆

DAILY QUOTE: *I choose to let go of the things I cannot control*

- Something nice I said to (*insert name*):

- How I feel about yesterday's progress:

- A setback or struggle I had:

- A win I had:

- A fear or concern I have:

- One positive thing that happened today:

- What I learned today:

TODAY'S ACTION LIST
Morning Prayer/Meditation ☐
Read Scripture/Recovery Lit ☐
Attended a Meeting ☐
Called Someone Sober ☐
Showered ☐ Teeth Brushed ☐
Water I Drank 1 2 3 4 5 6 7 8
Hours I Slept 1 2 3 4 5 6 7 8

TODAY I'M GRATEFUL FOR
1.
2.
3.

TODAY'S AGENDA	TIME

3 SELF-CARE THINGS I DID

MY RELATIONSHIPS CORNER

Date: _____ / _____ / _____ | **DAYS SOBER** | MOOD RATING: ☆☆☆☆☆

DAILY QUOTE: *I am worthy of a happy, healthy, and fulfilling life*

Something nice I said to (*insert name*):

How I feel about yesterday's progress:

A setback or struggle I had:

A win I had:

A fear or concern I have:

One positive thing that happened today:

What I learned today:

TODAY'S ACTION LIST
Morning Prayer/Meditation ☐
Read Scripture/Recovery Lit ☐
Attended a Meeting ☐
Called Someone Sober ☐
Showered ☐ Teeth Brushed ☐
Water I Drank   1 2 3 4 5 6 7 8
Hours I Slept   1 2 3 4 5 6 7 8

TODAY I'M GRATEFUL FOR
1. _____
2. _____
3. _____

TODAY'S AGENDA	TIME

3 SELF-CARE THINGS I DID

MY RELATIONSHIPS CORNER

Date: _____ / _____ / _____ | **DAYS SOBER** | MOOD RATING: ☆☆☆☆☆

DAILY QUOTE: *I am empowered to make positive changes in my life*

Something nice I said to (*insert name*):

How I feel about yesterday's progress:

A setback or struggle I had:

A win I had:

A fear or concern I have:

One positive thing that happened today:

What I learned today:

TODAY'S ACTION LIST
Morning Prayer/Meditation ☐
Read Scripture/Recovery Lit ☐
Attended a Meeting ☐
Called Someone Sober ☐
Showered ☐ Teeth Brushed ☐
Water I Drank   1 2 3 4 5 6 7 8
Hours I Slept   1 2 3 4 5 6 7 8

TODAY I'M GRATEFUL FOR
1. _____
2. _____
3. _____

TODAY'S AGENDA	TIME

3 SELF-CARE THINGS I DID

MY RELATIONSHIPS CORNER

Date: _____ / _____ / _____ | **DAYS SOBER** | MOOD RATING: ☆☆☆☆☆

DAILY QUOTE: *I am committed to my recovery, one day at a time*

- Something nice I said to (*insert name*):

- How I feel about yesterday's progress:

- A setback or struggle I had:

- A win I had:

- A fear or concern I have:

- One positive thing that happened today:

- What I learned today:

TODAY'S ACTION LIST
Morning Prayer/Meditation ☐
Read Scripture/Recovery Lit ☐
Attended a Meeting ☐
Called Someone Sober ☐
Showered ☐ Teeth Brushed ☐
Water I Drank   1 2 3 4 5 6 7 8
Hours I Slept   1 2 3 4 5 6 7 8

TODAY I'M GRATEFUL FOR
1. _____
2. _____
3. _____

TODAY'S AGENDA	TIME

3 SELF-CARE THINGS I DID

MY RELATIONSHIPS CORNER

Date: _____ / _____ / _____ | **DAYS SOBER** | MOOD RATING: ☆☆☆☆☆

DAILY QUOTE: *I choose to embrace self-love and positivity*

- Something nice I said to (*insert name*):

- How I feel about yesterday's progress:

- A setback or struggle I had:

- A win I had:

- A fear or concern I have:

- One positive thing that happened today:

- What I learned today:

TODAY'S ACTION LIST

Morning Prayer/Meditation ☐
Read Scripture/Recovery Lit ☐
Attended a Meeting ☐
Called Someone Sober ☐
Showered ☐ Teeth Brushed ☐
Water I Drank   1 2 3 4 5 6 7 8
Hours I Slept   1 2 3 4 5 6 7 8

TODAY I'M GRATEFUL FOR
1. _____
2. _____
3. _____

TODAY'S AGENDA	TIME

3 SELF-CARE THINGS I DID

MY RELATIONSHIPS CORNER

Date: _____ / _____ / _____ **DAYS SOBER** MOOD RATING: ☆☆☆☆☆

DAILY QUOTE: *I am proud of the person I am becoming*

Something nice I said to (*insert name*):

How I feel about yesterday's progress:

A setback or struggle I had:

A win I had:

A fear or concern I have:

One positive thing that happened today:

What I learned today:

TODAY'S ACTION LIST
Morning Prayer/Meditation ☐
Read Scripture/Recovery Lit ☐
Attended a Meeting ☐
Called Someone Sober ☐
Showered ☐ Teeth Brushed ☐
Water I Drank   1 2 3 4 5 6 7 8
Hours I Slept   1 2 3 4 5 6 7 8

TODAY I'M GRATEFUL FOR
1. _____
2. _____
3. _____

TODAY'S AGENDA	TIME

3 SELF-CARE THINGS I DID

MY RELATIONSHIPS CORNER

Date: _____ / _____ / _____ | **DAYS SOBER** | MOOD RATING: ☆☆☆☆☆

DAILY QUOTE: *I am learning to forgive myself and others*

Something nice I said to (*insert name*):

How I feel about yesterday's progress:

A setback or struggle I had:

A win I had:

A fear or concern I have:

One positive thing that happened today:

What I learned today:

TODAY'S ACTION LIST

Morning Prayer/Meditation ☐
Read Scripture/Recovery Lit ☐
Attended a Meeting ☐
Called Someone Sober ☐
Showered ☐ Teeth Brushed ☐
Water I Drank 1 2 3 4 5 6 7 8
Hours I Slept 1 2 3 4 5 6 7 8

TODAY I'M GRATEFUL FOR

1. _____
2. _____
3. _____

TODAY'S AGENDA	TIME

3 SELF-CARE THINGS I DID

MY RELATIONSHIPS CORNER

Date: _____ / _____ / _____ | **DAYS SOBER** | MOOD RATING: ☆☆☆☆☆

DAILY QUOTE: *I can overcome any challenge that comes my way*

Something nice I said to (*insert name*):

How I feel about yesterday's progress:

A setback or struggle I had:

A win I had:

A fear or concern I have:

One positive thing that happened today:

What I learned today:

TODAY'S ACTION LIST
Morning Prayer/Meditation ☐
Read Scripture/Recovery Lit ☐
Attended a Meeting ☐
Called Someone Sober ☐
Showered ☐   Teeth Brushed ☐
Water I Drank   1 2 3 4 5 6 7 8
Hours I Slept   1 2 3 4 5 6 7 8

TODAY I'M GRATEFUL FOR
1. _____
2. _____
3. _____

TODAY'S AGENDA	TIME

3 SELF-CARE THINGS I DID

MY RELATIONSHIPS CORNER

Date: _____ / _____ / _____ | **DAYS SOBER** | MOOD RATING: ☆☆☆☆☆

DAILY QUOTE: *I am learning to turn my vulnerabilities into strengths*

Something nice I said to (*insert name*):

How I feel about yesterday's progress:

A setback or struggle I had:

A win I had:

A fear or concern I have:

One positive thing that happened today:

What I learned today:

TODAY'S ACTION LIST
Morning Prayer/Meditation ☐
Read Scripture/Recovery Lit ☐
Attended a Meeting ☐
Called Someone Sober ☐
Showered ☐ Teeth Brushed ☐
Water I Drank   1 2 3 4 5 6 7 8
Hours I Slept   1 2 3 4 5 6 7 8

TODAY I'M GRATEFUL FOR
1. _____
2. _____
3. _____

TODAY'S AGENDA	TIME

3 SELF-CARE THINGS I DID

MY RELATIONSHIPS CORNER

Date: _____ / _____ / _____ | **DAYS SOBER** | MOOD RATING: ☆☆☆☆☆

DAILY QUOTE: *I am grateful for the small victories I have each day*

Something nice I said to (*insert name*):

How I feel about yesterday's progress:

A setback or struggle I had:

A win I had:

A fear or concern I have:

One positive thing that happened today:

What I learned today:

TODAY'S ACTION LIST
Morning Prayer/Meditation ☐
Read Scripture/Recovery Lit ☐
Attended a Meeting ☐
Called Someone Sober ☐
Showered ☐   Teeth Brushed ☐
Water I Drank   1 2 3 4 5 6 7 8
Hours I Slept   1 2 3 4 5 6 7 8

TODAY I'M GRATEFUL FOR
1. _____
2. _____
3. _____

TODAY'S AGENDA	TIME

3 SELF-CARE THINGS I DID

MY RELATIONSHIPS CORNER

Date: _____ / _____ / _____ **DAYS SOBER** MOOD RATING: ☆☆☆☆☆

DAILY QUOTE: *I choose to appreciate each moment in time*

Something nice I said to (*insert name*):

How I feel about yesterday's progress:

A setback or struggle I had:

A win I had:

A fear or concern I have:

One positive thing that happened today:

What I learned today:

TODAY'S ACTION LIST
Morning Prayer/Meditation ☐
Read Scripture/Recovery Lit ☐
Attended a Meeting ☐
Called Someone Sober ☐
Showered ☐ Teeth Brushed ☐
Water I Drank 1 2 3 4 5 6 7 8
Hours I Slept   1 2 3 4 5 6 7 8

TODAY I'M GRATEFUL FOR
1. _____
2. _____
3. _____

TODAY'S AGENDA	TIME

3 SELF-CARE THINGS I DID

MY RELATIONSHIPS CORNER

Date: _____ / _____ / _____ **DAYS SOBER** MOOD RATING: ☆☆☆☆☆

DAILY QUOTE: *I am worthy of respect and healthy relationships*

Something nice I said to (*insert name*):

How I feel about yesterday's progress:

A setback or struggle I had:

A win I had:

A fear or concern I have:

One positive thing that happened today:

What I learned today:

TODAY'S ACTION LIST

Morning Prayer/Meditation ☐
Read Scripture/Recovery Lit ☐
Attended a Meeting ☐
Called Someone Sober ☐
Showered ☐   Teeth Brushed ☐
Water I Drank   1 2 3 4 5 6 7 8
Hours I Slept   1 2 3 4 5 6 7 8

TODAY I'M GRATEFUL FOR

1.
2.
3.

TODAY'S AGENDA	TIME

3 SELF-CARE THINGS I DID

MY RELATIONSHIPS CORNER

Date: _____ / _____ / _____ | **DAYS SOBER** | MOOD RATING: ☆☆☆☆☆

DAILY QUOTE: *I am learning to find joy in the simple things in life*

Something nice I said to (*insert name*):

How I feel about yesterday's progress:

A setback or struggle I had:

A win I had:

A fear or concern I have:

One positive thing that happened today:

What I learned today:

TODAY'S ACTION LIST
Morning Prayer/Meditation ☐
Read Scripture/Recovery Lit ☐
Attended a Meeting ☐
Called Someone Sober ☐
Showered ☐ Teeth Brushed ☐
Water I Drank   1 2 3 4 5 6 7 8
Hours I Slept   1 2 3 4 5 6 7 8

TODAY I'M GRATEFUL FOR
1.
2.
3.

TODAY'S AGENDA	TIME

3 SELF-CARE THINGS I DID

MY RELATIONSHIPS CORNER

Date: _____ / _____ / _____ **DAYS SOBER**   MOOD RATING: ☆☆☆☆☆

DAILY QUOTE: *I am excited about what the future holds for me*

Something nice I said to (*insert name*):

How I feel about yesterday's progress:

A setback or struggle I had:

A win I had:

A fear or concern I have:

One positive thing that happened today:

What I learned today:

TODAY'S ACTION LIST

Morning Prayer/Meditation ☐
Read Scripture/Recovery Lit ☐
Attended a Meeting ☐
Called Someone Sober ☐
Showered ☐   Teeth Brushed ☐
Water I Drank   1 2 3 4 5 6 7 8
Hours I Slept   1 2 3 4 5 6 7 8

TODAY I'M GRATEFUL FOR

1. _____
2. _____
3. _____

TODAY'S AGENDA	TIME

3 SELF-CARE THINGS I DID

_____
_____
_____

MY RELATIONSHIPS CORNER

Date: _____ / _____ / _____ | DAYS SOBER | MOOD RATING: ☆☆☆☆☆

DAILY QUOTE: *I am learning to trust myself more each day*

- Something nice I said to (*insert name*):

- How I feel about yesterday's progress:

- A setback or struggle I had:

- A win I had:

- A fear or concern I have:

- One positive thing that happened today:

- What I learned today:

TODAY'S ACTION LIST

Morning Prayer/Meditation ☐
Read Scripture/Recovery Lit ☐
Attended a Meeting ☐
Called Someone Sober ☐
Showered ☐ Teeth Brushed ☐
Water I Drank   1 2 3 4 5 6 7 8
Hours I Slept   1 2 3 4 5 6 7 8

TODAY I'M GRATEFUL FOR

1. _____
2. _____
3. _____

TODAY'S AGENDA	TIME

3 SELF-CARE THINGS I DID

_____
_____
_____

MY RELATIONSHIPS CORNER

Date: _____ / _____ / _____   **DAYS SOBER** [_____]   MOOD RATING: ☆☆☆☆☆

DAILY QUOTE: *I am learning to find peace in the midst of chaos*

Something nice I said to (*insert name*):

How I feel about yesterday's progress:

A setback or struggle I had:

A win I had:

A fear or concern I have:

One positive thing that happened today:

What I learned today:

TODAY'S ACTION LIST
Morning Prayer/Meditation ☐
Read Scripture/Recovery Lit ☐
Attended a Meeting ☐
Called Someone Sober ☐
Showered ☐ Teeth Brushed ☐
Water I Drank 1 2 3 4 5 6 7 8
Hours I Slept   1 2 3 4 5 6 7 8

TODAY I'M GRATEFUL FOR
1. _____
2. _____
3. _____

TODAY'S AGENDA	TIME

3 SELF-CARE THINGS I DID

MY RELATIONSHIPS CORNER

Date: _____ / _____ / _____ | **DAYS SOBER** | MOOD RATING: ☆☆☆☆☆

DAILY QUOTE: *I am learning to appreciate and love myself*

Something nice I said to (*insert name*):

How I feel about yesterday's progress:

A setback or struggle I had:

A win I had:

A fear or concern I have:

One positive thing that happened today:

What I learned today:

TODAY'S ACTION LIST
Morning Prayer/Meditation ☐
Read Scripture/Recovery Lit ☐
Attended a Meeting ☐
Called Someone Sober ☐
Showered ☐ Teeth Brushed ☐
Water I Drank   1 2 3 4 5 6 7 8
Hours I Slept   1 2 3 4 5 6 7 8

TODAY I'M GRATEFUL FOR
1. _____
2. _____
3. _____

TODAY'S AGENDA	TIME

3 SELF-CARE THINGS I DID

MY RELATIONSHIPS CORNER

Date: _____ / _____ / _____ | **DAYS SOBER** | MOOD RATING: ☆☆☆☆☆

DAILY QUOTE: *I am grateful for the opportunities that come my way*

Something nice I said to (*insert name*):

How I feel about yesterday's progress:

A setback or struggle I had:

A win I had:

A fear or concern I have:

One positive thing that happened today:

What I learned today:

TODAY'S ACTION LIST
Morning Prayer/Meditation ☐
Read Scripture/Recovery Lit ☐
Attended a Meeting ☐
Called Someone Sober ☐
Showered ☐ Teeth Brushed ☐
Water I Drank 1 2 3 4 5 6 7 8
Hours I Slept 1 2 3 4 5 6 7 8

TODAY I'M GRATEFUL FOR
1. _____
2. _____
3. _____

TODAY'S AGENDA	TIME

3 SELF-CARE THINGS I DID

MY RELATIONSHIPS CORNER

Date: _____ / _____ / _____ | **DAYS SOBER** | MOOD RATING: ☆☆☆☆☆

DAILY QUOTE: *I am committed to living a life of purpose and meaning*

Something nice I said to (*insert name*):

How I feel about yesterday's progress:

A setback or struggle I had:

A win I had:

A fear or concern I have:

One positive thing that happened today:

What I learned today:

TODAY'S ACTION LIST
Morning Prayer/Meditation ☐
Read Scripture/Recovery Lit ☐
Attended a Meeting ☐
Called Someone Sober ☐
Showered ☐   Teeth Brushed ☐
Water I Drank   1 2 3 4 5 6 7 8
Hours I Slept   1 2 3 4 5 6 7 8

TODAY I'M GRATEFUL FOR
1.
2.
3.

TODAY'S AGENDA	TIME

3 SELF-CARE THINGS I DID

MY RELATIONSHIPS CORNER

The Imperative of Self-Care

Ah, self-care. The elusive concept that we all know we should be doing, but often put off for another day. Well, I'm here to tell you that self-care isn't just a buzzword – it's a very critical part of our recovery. So, get ready to learn how to give yourself some much-needed TLC.

First things first, WTF is self-care anyway? In short, it's any intentional action that we take to support our physical, mental, and emotional well-being. And no, that doesn't just mean indulging in our favorite pint of ice cream – although that can be a valid form of self-care from time to time which I have been known to use ☺.

Self-care can take many shapes and sizes. Maybe we're into yoga, or perhaps we prefer to sweat it out at the gym. Maybe we find peace in a good book, or perhaps we need to scream into a pillow to release some pent-up frustration. Whatever form it takes, self-care is all about making time for ourself and giving our mind, body, and soul the care and attention that they deserve.

The key to effective self-care is consistency. It's not enough to get a massage once a year and call it a day. We need to make self-care a regular part of our daily routine, and that means finding activities that we enjoy and that support our overall well-being.

We'll explore a variety of self-care practices to help support our recovery journey. From getting enough sleep and eating healthy, to self-compassion and self-exploration, to practicing mindfulness and engaging in fun activities, we'll find practical tips and exercises that we can incorporate into our daily routine.

So, let's get ready to finally make ourselves number one the right way and make our well-being a top priority. Remember, taking care of ourself isn't selfish – *it's essential!* Let's do this!

Why Self-Care is Crucial for Recovery

Okay, let's get real for a minute. Recovery is tough. I mean it's a rollercoaster of emotions, and sometimes it feels like we're barely hanging on by a thread. That's why self-care is crucial for those of us in recovery.

By the time we enter into recovery, our mind, body, and spirit have been through a lot. Addiction can take a toll on our physical health, our emotional well-being, and our relationships with others. Self-care is a way to start healing those wounds and rebuilding our life. But self-care isn't just a feel-good practice; it's actually essential for our recovery.

- <u>Stress Reduction:</u> Recovery can be stressful, both mentally and physically, and stress can trigger cravings and make it harder to stay on track. By practicing self-care, we can reduce our stress levels and improve our overall mood, making it a tad bit easier to stay on the path to recovery.
- <u>Improved Physical Health:</u> Addiction can take a toll on our body, and self-care practices like exercise, healthy eating, and getting enough sleep can help us to restore our physical health, stamina, and energy.
- <u>Better Mental Health:</u> Mental health is just as important as physical health when it comes to recovery. Self-care practices like meditation, journaling, and therapy can help us process our emotions and build a stronger sense of self-awareness.
- <u>Self-Compassion:</u> Addiction is usually accompanied by feelings of shame and self-blame. By practicing self-care, we're showing ourself compassion and kindness, which can help us build a more positive self-image and cultivate a healthier relationship with ourself.

In short, self-care is crucial for those of us in recovery because it supports our physical, mental, and emotional health and helps us build a strong foundation for long-term sobriety.

Practical Tips for Practicing Self-Care

1. <u>Take Care of Your Physical Health:</u> One of the best ways to practice self-care is to take care of our physical health. This can include getting enough sleep, eating a balanced and nutritious diet, and exercising regularly. When our body feels good, our mind will follow.
2. <u>Create a Daily Self-Care Routine:</u> Establishing a daily self-care routine can help us stay on track with our recovery and make self-care a regular part of our life. Our routine can be as simple as taking a few minutes each morning to meditate or journal, or as complex as a full morning routine that includes exercise, breakfast, and time for self-reflection.
3. <u>Build Strong Relationships:</u> Recovery can be a lonely journey, especially in the beginning. But building strong relationships with friends, family, and our support network can help us feel less isolated and more connected. Make time to connect with others regularly, whether it's through phone calls, support group meetings, or social activities. Especially when you don't feel like it!
4. <u>Cultivate a Hobby or Interest:</u> Finding a hobby or interest that we enjoy can be a great way to practice self-care and add more joy to our life. Whether

it's gardening, painting, playing an instrument, or coloring in a coloring book, finding an activity that brings us pleasure can help us feel more fulfilled and satisfied.
5. <u>Practice Mindfulness:</u> Mindfulness is the practice of being fully present in the moment, without judgment or distraction. Practicing mindfulness can help us stay grounded in the present and reduce feelings of anxiety or overwhelm. Try incorporating mindfulness practices like deep breathing, meditation, or mindful movement into a daily routine.

Self-care is a personal practice, and what works for one person may not work for another. The key is to experiment and find what self-care practices work best for each of us and incorporate them into our daily routine. By taking care of ourself, we're setting ourself up for a stronger, more resilient recovery.

Tip 1: Taking Care of Your Physical Health

Ah, yes, let's talk about the all-important task of taking care of our physical health. You know, that thing that's always on our to-do list, but somehow always gets pushed to the bottom. Well, it's time to prioritize it!

When we're in recovery, taking care of our physical health is essential. Our physical health affects our mental and emotional well-being, and vice versa. Which as we know, in turn, affects our cravings. In this section, we'll discuss some practical tips for taking care of our physical health and overcoming common roadblocks that we may encounter.

1. <u>Get Enough Sleep</u>

First things first, we need to make sure we're getting enough sleep. We all know how tough it is to fall asleep sometimes, and counting sheep certainly isn't the answer. Getting enough sleep is essential for our physical health and overall well-being. However, insomnia is a common problem for many people in addiction recovery. If we're having trouble sleeping, we can try:

- *Establish a regular sleep schedule*: We need to go to bed and get up at the same time every day, even on weekends. No matter how hard it is at first!
- *Create a relaxing sleep environment*: Keep the bedroom cool, dark, and quiet. Consider using a white noise machine or earplugs if we're sensitive to noise.
- *Avoid screens before bed*: The blue light emitted by screens can interfere with sleep. Avoid using electronic devices for at least an hour before bed.
- *Avoid caffeine and alcohol*: Both caffeine and alcohol can interfere with sleep. Avoid consuming them in the hours leading up to bedtime.
- *Create a night-time routine*: Try creating a soothing nighttime routine, like taking a warm bath or reading a book before bed.
- *Use a natural sleep aid*: Try incorporating some natural sleep aids, like chamomile tea or melatonin supplements.

If we continue to have trouble sleeping, we can always talk to our doctor or therapist. They may be able to provide additional support or resources to help us get the rest we need.

On a typical night, how many hours of sleep do you get? _____

Do you have trouble falling asleep or staying asleep? If so, what have you tried?

_____
_____
_____
_____

Do your sleep habits have a significant impact on your mood and energy levels throughout the day?

_____
_____
_____
_____
_____
_____

Have you tried incorporating any relaxation or mindfulness techniques into your bedtime routine? If so, which ones have been most helpful?

_____
_____
_____
_____
_____

Do you use electronic devices (phone/computer) just before bed? _____

If so, have you noticed any negative effects on your sleep or overall well-being?

_____
_____
_____
_____
_____
_____
_____

2. Eat a Balanced and Nutritious Diet

Now, let's move on to the dreaded topic of diet. Who has time to count calories and measure out portions? Ain't nobody got time for that shit! But that doesn't mean we should let our diet go completely off the rails. Especially now when our body is trying to recuperate from the all the damage that we've done to it.

Eating a balanced and nutritious diet is essential for our physical health. However, it can be challenging to know what a balanced diet actually looks like, especially if we're used to relying on our addiction for sustenance.

- *Whole foods*: Whole foods are minimally processed and rich in nutrients. Examples include fruits, vegetables, whole grains, lean protein, and healthy fats such as olives and avocados and their oils.
- *Limit processed and packaged foods*: These foods are often high in salt, sugar, and unhealthy fats, and usually lack important nutrients. Plus, they have been known to make people feel sluggish.
- *Drink plenty of water*: Staying hydrated is essential for overall health. It flushes out toxins and helps to deliver nutrients throughout our body. Aim to drink at least eight glasses of water per day.
- *Avoid skipping meals*: Skipping meals can lead to overeating or unhealthy food choices later in the day. Plus, the body and brain need fuel to function.
- *Prep food ahead*: If cooking isn't your thing, try prepping some healthy meals and snacks in advance, like salads, sliced veggies and hummus or trail mix.

If we're unsure about what a balanced diet should look like for our particular body, we can always talk to a registered dietitian. They can provide us with personalized guidance and support to help us establish healthy eating habits for ourselves.

How has your diet and nutrition played a role in your recovery journey?

_____
_____
_____
_____
_____
_____

What steps can you take to ensure that you are fueling your body with the nutrients it needs to thrive?

_____
_____
_____
_____
_____

3. <u>Exercise Regularly</u>

Exercise is a great natural mood booster, and it doesn't have to be a full-on, intense workout. Just a quick walk outside or some gentle yoga can do wonders.

Exercise is an essential part of physical health, and it can also help improve our mood and reduce feelings of anxiety and depression (which we seem prone to). However, getting started with exercise can be challenging, especially if we're dealing with physical or mental health issues.

- *Start slow*: Begin with a low-impact exercise, such as walking or swimming, and gradually increase the intensity over time with your doctor's guidance.
- *Find an exercise buddy*: Having a friend or accountability partner can help us to stay motivated and committed to an exercise routine. Plus, everything is better with a buddy to do it with.
- *Try different types of exercise*: Experiment with different types of exercise, such as yoga, strength training, or dance. Find an activity that you enjoy and look forward to.
- *Be kind to yourself*: Don't push yourself too hard or beat yourself up if you miss a workout. Be patient and compassionate with yourself as you establish a new routine.

What physical activities do you do to take care of your physical health?

_____
_____
_____
_____
_____
_____
_____
_____

What activities would you like to start or incorporate into your routine?

_____
_____
_____
_____
_____
_____
_____
_____

4. Manage Chronic Health Conditions

And finally, let's talk about managing chronic health conditions. It's not fun, but it's necessary. We need to work with our healthcare provider to come up with a plan that works for us, whether that's medication management or lifestyle changes. And don't forget, managing chronic health conditions can also play a role in addiction recovery. By reducing pain or other symptoms, we can reduce our cravings thereby reducing the risk of relapse.

If we're dealing with a chronic health condition, it's essential to manage it as part of our overall physical health. We need to work with our qualified doctor on this. We should talk to our doctor about our health condition and develop a treatment plan that works for us without jeopardizing our recovery.

Overall, taking care of our physical health might seem overwhelming, but it doesn't have to be. Just take it one step at a time, and remember that small changes can make a big difference.

Tip 2: Create a Daily Self-Care Routine

Ah, the daily grind. It can be tough to carve out some time for ourself in the midst of work, family, and other responsibilities. But trust me, it's worth it. Creating a daily self-care routine can help us stay centered and calm, even in the midst of chaos.

First things first, let's make a list of activities that make us feel good. Maybe it's taking a long walk, practicing yoga, or reading a good book. Whatever it is, write it down.

Some activities that I enjoy:

_____ | _____
_____ | _____
_____ | _____

Now, we can create a schedule that incorporates these activities into our day or week. It doesn't have to be a huge time commitment - even just 15-30 minutes a day can make a big difference.

	Activity One	Activity Two
Monday		
Tuesday		
Wednesday		
Thursday		
Friday		
Saturday		
Sunday		

Of course, there will be roadblocks along the way. Maybe we have a busy work schedule, or we're feeling too tired to get out of bed in the morning. That's okay.

- *Wake up a little earlier.* I know, I know - sleep is important. But getting up just 15 minutes earlier can give you some extra time to fit in those self-care activities.
- *Use your lunch break.* Instead of mindlessly scrolling through TikTok, use the lunch break to take a walk or practice some meditation.
- *Take advantage of technology.* There are tons of apps out there that can help you stay on track with your self-care routine. From meditation apps to fitness trackers, find what works for you and stick with it.
- *Enlist the help of a friend.* Maybe you and a friend can go for a walk or practice yoga together. Having someone to hold you accountable can make all the difference.

Now, let's talk about what a daily self-care routine might look like.

- *Start your day with a mindfulness practice.* This could be as simple as taking a few deep breaths or practicing a quick meditation.
- *Move your body.* Whether it's a yoga class, a jog around the block, or a dance party in your living room, getting your body moving can help you feel energized and focused.
- *Take breaks throughout the day.* Instead of staring at your computer or cell phone for hours on end, take a quick break every hour or so to stretch, take a walk, or do some deep breathing.
- *Unplug before bed.* Turn off your phone and other devices at least 30 minutes before bed to give your brain a chance to wind down.
- *Get a good night's sleep.* Make sure you're getting enough rest - aim for 6-8 hours a night if possible.

Creating a daily self-care routine can seem daunting, but it doesn't have to be. Just start with one small thing and build from there. And remember, taking care of ourself isn't selfish - *it's necessary!*

What are some potential roadblocks you face in practicing self-care?

_____
_____
_____
_____
_____
_____
_____
_____
_____
_____

How can you overcome these obstacles?

___

How can you create a daily self-care routine that fits into your existing schedule and helps you prioritize your physical, emotional, and mental well-being?

___

Tip 3: Build Strong Relationships

As humans, we are social creatures. We thrive on interaction, connection, and a sense of belonging. That's why building strong relationships is a crucial part of any recovery journey.

But let's be real. If we're in recovery, chances are we've caused some serious damage to some of the most important relationships in our life. Maybe we hurt our partner, distanced ourself from our family, or lost touch with good friends. Rebuilding those relationships might seem impossible, but it's not. It does, however, take time, patience, and a willingness to do the work.

- *Take Responsibility*: It's important for us to take responsibility for our past actions and acknowledge the harm we may have caused. We need to be sincere in our apologies and show that we are committed to making things right.
- *Be Patient*: Rebuilding trust takes time. Don't expect things to be fixed overnight. Let's be patient and consistent in our efforts.

- *Communicate Openly*: Communication is key in any relationship. We have to be open and honest with our loved ones about our recovery journey, our struggles, and our successes.
- *Make Amends*: If we've hurt someone, it's important to make amends. This doesn't mean just saying sorry. It means taking action to repair the damage we've done. (We'll cover this more fully later in the book)
- *Create Boundaries*: Sometimes, relationships can be toxic. It's important for us to create boundaries and remove ourself from situations or people that may trigger us or cause us harm.

Now, let's talk about roadblocks. Rebuilding relationships can be tough, especially if our loved ones are hesitant or unwilling to forgive. It's important to remember that we can only control our own actions, not the actions of others.

- *Practice Self-Compassion*: Recovery is a journey, and there will be bumps in the road. Be kind to yourself and remember that you're doing the best you can with what you have.
- *Seek Support*: Lean on your sponsor, support group, or therapist for guidance and support. They can offer a different perspective and help you navigate difficult situations.
- *Be Patient*: Rebuilding trust takes time. It's important to be patient and consistent in your efforts to rebuild relationships.
- *Make New Connections*: Building new relationships with others in recovery can help you feel less isolated and more connected. Attend support group meetings or get involved in sober activities.

Building strong relationships in recovery is crucial to our overall well-being. It takes time, effort, and a willingness to do the work. But in the end, the rewards far outweigh the work. We'll feel less alone, more connected, and have a support system to help us through the tough times.

Listen up, building new relationships in recovery can be a whole lot easier than we might think. And let's face it, who better to relate to our struggles and triumphs than our fellow recovering addicts and alcoholics? So, let's dive in and make those connections and build a strong recovery team.

First off, don't be shy – we should put ourself out there! Attend meetings and recovery events, and don't be afraid to introduce ourself to others. We might be surprised at how many people are willing to share their stories and offer support. Remember, they've been there, done that too!

But don't stop there - take the initiative to connect with others outside of meetings too. Maybe suggest grabbing coffee or lunch with a fellow member, or attend a sober activity together. And if we're struggling with social anxiety or fear of rejection, remember that most people in recovery were or are just as nervous as we are.

And let's not forget about our recovery team beyond our fellow alcoholics and addicts. This can include therapists, sponsors, doctors, and other healthcare providers. We should never be afraid to ask for help when we need it, and always keep an open line of communication with our team.

But what if we're struggling with building new relationships due to past traumas or social anxiety? It's important to address those roadblocks in therapy or with a trusted friend or sponsor. They can help us work through those issues and provide support along the way.

And lastly, remember the importance of self-care in building and maintaining relationships. We need to prioritize taking care of ourself so that we can be present and engaged in our interactions with others.

So, go ahead and put yourself out there. Building new relationships in recovery can be scary, but the rewards are endless. And who knows, we might just make some lifelong friends along the way.

Who are the people in your life that you consider as part of your recovery team?

_____
_____
_____
_____
_____
_____
_____

How do they support your well-being?

_____
_____
_____
_____
_____
_____
_____

How can you strengthen these relationships further?

_____
_____
_____
_____
_____
_____
_____
_____

Tip 4: Cultivate a Hobby or Interest

Now, let's talk about why cultivating a hobby or interest is crucial for those of us in recovery. First and foremost, having a hobby or interest can help us fill our time with something positive and fulfilling. Instead of dwelling on past mistakes or feeling bored which brings on cravings, we can channel our energy into something productive and enjoyable.

Plus, having a hobby or interest can help us build a sense of identity outside of our addiction. We are so much more than just our past mistakes and struggles! By exploring new interests and hobbies, we can discover new aspects of ourselves and build a more positive self-image. So, what are some hobbies or interests you could try out? Here are just a few ideas to help get you started:

- Photography
- Writing
- Painting or drawing
- Gardening
- Yoga or meditation
- Cooking or baking
- Reading
- Traveling
- Knitting or crocheting
- Hiking or exploring nature
- Playing sports or exercising
- Learning to play an instrument
- Volunteering in your community
- Taking a class or workshop that interests you
- Coloring in a coloring book (yes, I'm serious - it's a great way to relieve stress and anxiety)

And don't forget, we don't have to do any of these alone. Cultivating a hobby or interest can also be a great way to connect with others who share our passions. Whether it's joining a hiking group or taking a cooking class, there are plenty of ways to build new relationships through our hobbies and interests.

But I know it's not always easy to get started. Maybe we're feeling overwhelmed or don't know where to begin. Or maybe we're worried about the cost or time commitment of a new hobby.

- *Start small* - don't feel like you have to become an expert overnight. Start by setting aside just a few minutes a day to work on your hobby or interest.
- *Look for free or low-cost options* - there are plenty of hobbies that don't cost a lot of money or even any money to get started. For example, hiking is free and writing can be done with just a pen and paper and a bit of imagination.
- *Don't be afraid to try something new* - it's okay if you're not immediately great at something. Give yourself permission to experiment and make mistakes.
- *Find a friend to do it with* - not only can this help hold you accountable, but it can also make the experience more enjoyable and less intimidating.

Cultivating a hobby or interest can be a great way to boost our overall sense of well-being and build new relationships in recovery. Plus, we might discover a new passion that brings us joy for many years to come. I know I did!

What hobbies or interests do you currently have?

_____
_____
_____

How do they contribute to your overall sense of well-being?

Are there any new hobbies or interests you'd like to explore?

Tip 5: Practice Mindfulness

Hey, you've made it to tip number 5. Congratulations, *you're killing it!*

Alright, it's time to stop living on autopilot and start living in the now. That's right, we're talking about mindfulness. Mindfulness is about paying attention to the present moment, and it's a crucial part of recovery. It can help us stay focused on our goals, reduce stress and anxiety, and improve our overall well-being. So, let's talk about some of the ways we can practice mindfulness.

- *Meditation*: Find a quiet place to sit, close your eyes, and focus on your breath. If your mind starts to wander, gently bring it back to your breath.
- *Mindful breathing*: Take a few minutes to focus on your breath. Feel the air coming in and out of your body.
- *Body scan*: Lie down and bring your attention to each part of your body, from your toes to the top of your head.
- *Mindful eating*: Slow down and savor each bite of your food. Pay attention to the texture, taste, and smell.
- *Mindful walking*: Take a walk and pay attention to the sights, sounds, and sensations around you.
- *Gratitude practice*: Take a few moments each day to think about something you're grateful for.
- *Journaling*: Write down your thoughts and feelings.
- *Yoga*: Practice yoga and focus on the movements and your breath.
- *Mindful listening*: Focus on the person who is speaking and really listen to what they're saying.
- *Mindful self-compassion*: Practice being kind and understanding to yourself, especially during difficult times.

And if you're struggling to practice mindfulness, don't worry, you're not alone. Here are some common barriers and ways to overcome them:

- *Time*: It can be challenging to find time to practice mindfulness, especially if you have a busy schedule. Start small by setting aside just a few minutes each day to focus on your breath or practice a body scan.
- *Distractions*: It's easy to get distracted by noise, technology, and other things that demand our attention. Try to find a quiet place to practice mindfulness, or use headphones to block out distractions.
- *Resistance*: You might feel resistant to practicing mindfulness because it feels uncomfortable or unfamiliar. Remember that it takes time to build a new habit, and be gentle with yourself as you work on incorporating mindfulness into your daily routine.

Mindfulness is a powerful tool for recovery, and with a little practice, anyone can learn to live in the present moment, even us! The next chapter is dedicated to mindfulness practices.

How does practicing mindfulness help you in your recovery?

What specific mindfulness practices have you tried?

How have they impacted your well-being?

Mindfulness Practices

First things first, mindfulness is basically the art of paying attention on purpose. It's a skill that we can cultivate, which allows us to be more present in the moment and aware of our thoughts and emotions.

Now, you might be thinking, *"But wait, isn't paying attention something we all do naturally?"* Well, sort of. We're always processing information from our environment, but we're not always aware of what's going on in our minds. In fact, our minds can be incredibly noisy and chaotic, jumping from one thought to another without any real direction. Especially for us addicts!

Mindfulness helps us to cut through that noise and focus our attention on what's happening in the present moment. It's not about getting rid of thoughts or trying to force ourselves to be calm. It's about accepting what's happening in the moment and being aware of it without judgment.

There are many different techniques that can help us practice mindfulness, such as meditation, deep breathing, body scans, and mindful movement. The key is to find what works for each of us and make it a regular part of our routine.

But why bother with mindfulness in the first place? Well, there are many benefits to practicing mindfulness, including:

- Reduced stress and anxiety
- Improved mental clarity & focus
- Increased self-awareness
- Increased self-acceptance
- Better sleep
- Enhanced relationships with others

Basically, mindfulness can help us to be more present and engaged in our lives, which in turn can lead to greater happiness and fulfillment.

While mindfulness seems to be a buzzword these days, we can't let that fool us into thinking it's some sort of new trendy fad. Mindfulness has been around for thousands of years and is a powerful tool for addiction recovery amongst other things. It's all about being in the present and fully engaged in the current moment, not getting bogged down in the past or worrying about the future. And let's face it, when we're in addiction recovery, staying in the present moment can be a real challenge!

So why is mindfulness so essential for addiction recovery? Well, let's break it down.

First and foremost, mindfulness helps us manage our cravings and urges. By being fully present and aware of our thoughts and emotions, we can catch ourselves when we start to feel triggered and take a step back to analyze what's happening in our minds. This can help us make more rational decisions and avoid falling back into old, unhealthy habits.

Mindfulness also helps us build resilience in the face of stress and difficult emotions. When we're in addiction recovery, there will be some pretty tough moments. By practicing mindfulness regularly, we can learn to accept those moments and approach them with a sense of calm and openness, rather than the panic and resistance that we're used to.

Another reason mindfulness is essential for addiction recovery is that it helps us develop a deeper sense of self-awareness. By paying attention to our own thoughts, emotions, and physical sensations, we can start to recognize patterns and triggers that we may not have noticed before. This can help us make more informed decisions and develop a greater sense of self-control.

Finally, mindfulness helps us cultivate a sense of gratitude and appreciation for the present moment. When we're in addiction recovery, it's easy to get bogged down in all the negative shit of our situation. By practicing mindfulness and focusing on the good things in our lives, we can shift our perspective and start to see the world in a more positive light. Yay!

Mindfulness is an essential tool for addiction recovery because it helps us manage our cravings and urges, build resilience in the face of stress and difficult emotions, develop self-awareness, and cultivate a sense of gratitude and appreciation. And let's not forget that mindfulness is also just a damn good way to improve our overall well-being.

Now, let's get into some actionable ways we can practice mindfulness.

- *Mindful breathing*: This is where you take a few minutes to focus on your breath. Pay attention to the sensation of the air moving in and out of your body. When your mind starts to wander (as it inevitably will), gently bring your attention back to your breath.
- *Body scan meditation*: This is where you take some time to focus on different parts of your body, one at a time, and notice the physical sensations in your body. This can help you to get more in tune with your body.
- *Mindful walking*: Instead of walking anywhere on autopilot, you can take a few minutes to really pay attention to your surroundings. This can be a great way to clear your mind and feel more grounded.
- *Mindful eating*: When you eat, take the time to pay attention to the flavors and textures. This can help the meal seem more delightful and help you feel more satisfied.
- *Guided meditations*: These types of meditations can be a great way to get started with mindfulness or to mix things up if you're feeling stuck.

Of course, practicing mindfulness isn't always easy. We all have our barriers and roadblocks, whether it's a busy schedule, a wandering mind, or other distractions.

- *Set aside dedicated time*: Carve out time each day to practice mindfulness, even if it's just a few minutes. Make it a non-negotiable part of your routine.
- *Start small*: Don't try to go from zero to 60 with mindfulness. Start with just a few minutes a day and gradually work your way up.
- *Eliminate distractions*: Find a quiet, peaceful space where you won't be interrupted. Turn off your phone and other devices so you can focus fully on the present moment.
- *Use guided meditations*: If you're struggling to quiet your mind, try using guided meditations to help you focus and stay present.
- *Practice throughout the day*: Mindfulness doesn't have to be limited to your dedicated practice time. Try to incorporate mindfulness into your everyday activities, like washing dishes or taking a shower.
- *Be kind to yourself*: Don't beat yourself up if your mind wanders or you have a hard time staying present. Mindfulness is a skill, and like any skill, it takes practice and patience to improve.
- *Don't give up*: If you miss a day or have a setback, don't let it discourage you. Just pick up where you left off and keep practicing.

Remember, mindfulness is a practice, and like any practice, it takes time and dedication to see the benefits. Let's be patient with ourselves – I know, I know, a new concept! If we keep practicing, we'll start to see improvements in our overall well-being and our addiction recovery. Ready to dive in and start practicing? Let's go!

Exercise 1: Mindful Breathing

Let's begin with the old classic: Mindful Breathing.

First, find a comfortable position. Sit in a chair or on a cushion, cross-legged or not. Just make sure you're comfortable enough to sit for a full few minutes without fidgeting. Close your eyes or lower your gaze. This helps to eliminate visual distractions and allows you to focus on your breath.

Begin to breathe naturally. Don't force your breath, just breathe normally. Focus on your breath. Start to pay attention to the sensation of your breath as it moves in and out of your body. Notice the rising and falling of your chest or belly and the air moving through your nostrils.

If your mind wanders, gently bring it back to your breath. Your mind will inevitably wander off to other thoughts or distractions. That's normal. Just gently acknowledge the thought and then bring your attention back to your breath.

Keep breathing and focusing on your breath. Do this for a few minutes or for as long as you like. Some people like to set a timer for five or ten minutes. When you're finished, take a few deep breaths and then open your eyes or lift your gaze.

So that's mindful breathing. Remember, it's called a mindfulness *practice* for a reason. Don't worry if it feels difficult or if your mind wanders a lot. The more you do it, the easier it will become.

Here are reflection questions after practicing mindful breathing to help us reflect on our experience and identify any obstacles or opportunities for growth as we continue to practice mindfulness.

How did you feel during the exercise?

_____
_____
_____
_____
_____
_____

Were you able to focus on your breath, or did your mind wander?

_____
_____
_____
_____
_____

If your mind wandered, what brought your attention back to your breath?

_____
_____
_____
_____
_____

Did you notice physical sensations, emotions, or thoughts during the exercise?

_____
_____
_____
_____
_____

Do you think you can include mindful breathing in your daily routine?

What benefits do you think you could gain from using mindful breathing daily?

What challenges do you think you'll face in using mindful breathing on the reg?

How can you address them and keep a consistent mindfulness practice?

Exercise 2: Body Scan Meditation

Now we are going to learn how to do a body scan. This is a practice where you focus on different parts of your body, one at a time, and notice any physical sensations or feelings that arise. It can be a great way to release tension and get more in tune with your body.

First, find a comfortable spot to sit or lie down. You don't want to be distracted by discomfort or cramps when you're trying to focus on your body. Once you're settled, it's time to start the body scan.

Start at your toes, wiggle them a bit to get them feeling awake, and then focus your attention on them. Imagine that you're sending your breath down to your toes, and as you inhale, you're filling them with fresh oxygen. As you exhale, imagine that you're releasing any tension or discomfort that might be there. Stay with your toes for a minute or two, then move up to your feet and repeat the process.

Keep working your way up your body, part by part, until you've scanned everything from your toes to your head. It's important to stay focused on each area for a minute or two, really taking the time to feel the sensations in your body. If you notice any tension or discomfort, try to breathe into that area and imagine releasing the tension with every exhale.

If your mind starts to wander (which, let's be honest, is probably going to happen), gently bring it back to the part of your body you were focusing on. Don't judge yourself for getting distracted; it's a natural part of the process. Just refocus and keep going.

When you've finished the body scan, take a few deep breaths and stretch your body a bit. Notice how you feel - hopefully more relaxed and in tune with your physical self.

Congratulations, you just did a body scan meditation!

What did you notice during the Body Scan Meditation?

_____
_____
_____
_____
_____
_____

Did you find it challenging to keep your focus on your body and your breath?

_____
_____
_____
_____
_____

Did you notice any physical sensations or areas of tension in your body that you hadn't been aware of before?

_____
_____
_____
_____
_____
_____

Did you notice any thoughts or emotions that arose during the meditation?

_____
_____
_____
_____
_____
_____

If so, how did you respond to them?

_____
_____
_____
_____
_____
_____

Did you feel more relaxed or grounded after the Body Scan Meditation?

_____
_____
_____
_____
_____
_____

If so, how could you include this each day or week to help you manage stress and anxiety?

_____
_____
_____
_____
_____
_____
_____
_____
_____

Exercise 3: Mindful Walking

This one is great for those of us who don't want to sit still, because let's be honest, who wants to do that all the time? Instead of walking from point A to point B on autopilot, we are going to take a few minutes to really pay attention to our surroundings. We want to notice the sights, sounds, and smells around us as well as the sensations of the air like the wind or the sun on our face. This can be a great way for us to get some clarity and feel more grounded. Here's how to do a mindful walking meditation in all its glory:

First, find a quiet, peaceful place where you can walk without distractions. If you're in a city, try to find a park or somewhere with trees and nature. If you're in the middle of nowhere, congratulations! You have the perfect place already.

Now we are going to just stand still and take a few deep breaths. Notice how your feet feel on the ground and how your body feels standing upright.

Start walking slowly, paying attention to each step. Notice how your feet feel as they lift off the ground, move through the air, and land on the ground again.

As you walk, try to focus on your breath too. Take deep breaths in and out, feeling your lungs expand and contract. Pay attention to your surroundings. Notice the colors, the textures, the sounds, and the smells. Feel the sun on your skin or the wind in your hair.

If your mind starts to wander (and it will), gently bring it back to the present moment. Don't get mad at yourself for wandering thoughts, just notice it and come back to your breath and your steps.

Keep walking and breathing mindfully for as long as you'd like. You can set a timer or just go until you feel ready to stop. When you're done, stop and take a few deep breaths again. Notice how your body feels after the meditation, and how your mind feels more calm and focused.

And there you have it, a mindful walking meditation that you can do just about anywhere (as long as it's safe to walk, of course). So put on your walking shoes and get out there!

How did you feel during the mindful walking exercise?

Did you notice any sensations in your body? If so, what were they?

Were you able to stay focused in the present or did your mind wander?

Did you find mindful walking to help you feel more relaxed or less stressed?

Was it difficult to stay present during the exercise?

_____
_____
_____
_____
_____
_____
_____

If so, what were some of the challenges you faced?

_____
_____
_____
_____
_____
_____
_____
_____

Did you notice any changes in your mood or energy after mindful walking?

_____
_____
_____
_____
_____
_____
_____
_____

How can you incorporate mindful walking into your regular routine, even when you're busy or on-the-go?

___

Do you have any additional insights or observations about your experience?

___

Exercise 4: Mindful Eating

Ah, mindful eating. It's the art of paying attention to what we're stuffing in our face hole, without getting distracted by the latest cat video on YouTube. Seriously though, when we eat, we take the time to really savor the food and pay attention to the aromas, flavors, and textures. This can help make the food we eat become more enjoyable and help us to feel more satisfied and less likely to eat too much. Here's how to do it:

Pick a time to eat when you're not rushed or distracted. Turn off the TV, put down your phone, and focus on the food in front of you.

Before even taking the first bite, take a moment to appreciate the colors, smells, and textures of your food. Really savor the aroma, like you're some kind of fancy-pants food critic.

Now, take a bite and chew slowly. Don't just mindlessly chomp away. Instead, roll it around your tongue and really taste the food. Notice how the flavors and textures change as you chew.

Pay attention to your body's signals. Are you getting full? Do you feel satisfied? Are you still hungry? Tune in to your body's needs and respond to them accordingly.

Repeat these steps for the rest of your meal, enjoying and savoring every bite and really taking the time to appreciate the food in front of you.

Just remember, no distractions, really savor the food, chew slowly, pay attention to your body, and enjoy the experience. Bon appétit!

Reflecting on the following questions can help deepen our awareness of our eating habits and patterns, and identify areas where we may want to make changes. It can also help us become more attuned to our body's signals of hunger and fullness, which can support more mindful and *intuitive* eating.

What did you notice during the practice?

Were there any physical sensations, emotions, or thoughts that came up?

How did the food taste and feel in your mouth?

Did you notice any textures or flavors you hadn't before?

_____
_____
_____
_____
_____

Did you find yourself slowing down while eating?

_____
_____
_____
_____
_____

Did you take smaller bites and chew your food more thoroughly?

_____
_____
_____
_____
_____

Did you eat the entire portion of food or did you find yourself feeling satisfied and stopping before finishing?

_____
_____
_____
_____
_____

How did you feel after the practice?

___

Did you feel connected to your body and senses, or present in the moment?

___

Exercise 5: Guided meditations

Get ready for a journey through the inner sanctum of your mind, led by a calm, soothing voice that will guide you to relaxation and self-awareness. This one is my favorite! All you need is a quiet space, comfortable seating, and maybe some headphones if you want to fully immerse yourself in the experience (which would be my suggestion).

To begin, find a guided meditation that speaks to you. There are plenty of guided meditations available online or through apps like Calm and Headspace that offer free or paid guided meditations on a variety of topics. You will also find free guided meditations on YouTube. Take the time to check out several and choose one that aligns with your intentions or simply pick one that resonates with you. For a quick meditation break, I personally prefer this site: www.orindaben.com/pages/rooms/orin_meditation_room.

Once you've found your guided meditation, sit or lie down in a comfortable position and hit play. As the voice begins to speak, focus on your breath and allow yourself to relax into the present moment.

The voice will likely guide you through a series of visualizations, breathing exercises, and prompts to help you tap into your inner world. Follow along and let your mind go where it needs to go. Don't worry if your thoughts wander or if you find it hard to concentrate at first - this is all part of the process. I fell asleep the first few times I did a guided meditation.

Allow yourself to fully immerse in the guided meditation and let it take you on a journey through your thoughts and emotions. You may find that you feel more relaxed, centered, and in tune with your inner self after the meditation.

So, what are you waiting for? Give guided meditation a try and see where it takes you. Just don't forget to come back to reality when it's over!

How did you feel during the guided meditation?

_____
_____
_____
_____
_____
_____
_____
_____
_____

Did you notice any changes in your body or mind?

_____
_____
_____
_____
_____
_____
_____
_____
_____

What thoughts or emotions came up during the meditation?

_____
_____
_____
_____
_____
_____
_____
_____
_____

Were there any particular moments that stood out to you?

Did you find it easy or difficult to follow the instructions in the meditation?

What was most helpful about the guided meditation?

Was there anything that you struggled with?

After the meditation, how do you feel? More relaxed or energized?

Would you use this guided meditation again? If so, when and where?

Are there any other types of guided meditations you'd like to try in the future?

How do you think you could include guided meditation into your daily routine?

___

Did you have any trouble staying focused during the guided meditation?

___

If so, what strategies might you use in the future to stay more present?

___

How did this guided meditation compare to other meditations you've tried?

___

Identifying and Managing Triggers

Ah, triggers. Those pesky little things that can creep up on us and send us spiraling back into old habits. It's like they're trying to sabotage us, am I right?

But seriously, we all know that identifying and managing triggers is an essential part of addiction recovery. It's important to know what kinds of situations, people, and emotions might set off that little voice in our heads that tells us to reach for our addiction. It's like we need a trigger radar, or a personal trigger alert system.

Triggers can be all sorts of things. Maybe it's a certain place, like a bar or a party where everyone is drinking. Maybe it's a certain person, like an old drinking buddy or an ex who always made you feel like you needed to drink to cope. Maybe it's a certain feeling, like loneliness or boredom or stress, that always seemed to lead you down a dark path.

The thing is, triggers can be sneaky. They can show up when we least expect them, and sometimes they can even disguise themselves as something else entirely. Like, maybe you think you're just stressed out from work, but really, it's a trigger that's making you want to drink or use.

That's why it's so important to be aware of our triggers and to have a plan for managing them. We can't always avoid them completely, but we can learn how to recognize them and cope with them in healthy ways.

Recognizing Triggers

First of all, let's define what we mean by "triggers". Triggers are those things that set off a chain reaction in our brains, leading us to crave the substance or behavior that we're trying to avoid. Triggers can be anything from a certain place or person to a specific emotion or situation.

Recognizing our triggers is a process that requires self-awareness, honesty, and openness to discovering new insights about ourselves. It can be easy to assume that we already know all of our triggers, but the truth is that we might be overlooking some very important ones.

For example, some triggers might be obvious, such as being around certain people or in certain environments. But there might be more subtle triggers that we aren't as aware of, such as specific emotions or our thought patterns.

What are some of your obvious triggers?

_____
_____
_____
_____
_____
_____
_____
_____

What are some of your more subtle triggers?

_____
_____
_____
_____
_____
_____
_____

It can also be helpful to remember that triggers can change over time, so it's important to stay attuned to what might be setting off our addictive behaviors at any given moment. This requires ongoing self-reflection and a willingness to be curious and explore our experiences with a non-judgmental attitude.

Have you noticed any of your triggers changing? What ones changed?

_____
_____
_____
_____
_____
_____

So, if you're in recovery, it's important to stay open to learning more about yourself and your triggers. Don't assume that you already know everything there is to know. Instead, approach the process with an open mind and a willingness to learn and grow.

So, how do we recognize triggers? One approach is to use the acronym H.A.L.T. which stands for Hungry, Angry, Lonely, Tired. These are four common emotional states that can trigger cravings and lead to slips or relapse. So, if we're feeling any of these things, it's important to recognize that we may be more vulnerable in that moment and take steps to protect our recovery.

Another way to recognize triggers is to keep a trigger journal. I call this a *trigger tracker* and I include one in a few of my workbooks as well as having a couple of stand-alone trigger trackers. I also include one at the back of this workbook just for us!

A trigger tracker is pretty simple to use, you just write down the situations or emotions that you're in when you experience cravings. The other questions such as when the trigger happened, what you were doing or thinking, and who you were with when you experienced a craving, slip, or relapse, can help you to identify patterns as well as triggers that you may not have been aware of before.

Using a trigger tracker can be really helpful for us to not only identify our triggers but also track them over time and see patterns that we may not have noticed before. It can also help us to develop coping strategies that are tailored to specific triggers. Plus, it's a great excuse to buy a fancy new journal (wink, wink 😊😊).

Tracking our mood can be another helpful tool in identifying triggers because it can give us insights into our behavior and help us to identify patterns. Try using a mood chart or simply set aside a couple of minutes for a daily mood check-in.

A mood chart is a visual tool that allows us to track our mood over time. We can create our own chart using a simple graph or use a pre-made template.

A daily check-in is like a journal where we write in our thoughts and feelings each day which can help us to identify patterns in our mood and behavior. Set aside a few minutes each day to reflect on your mood and how you're feeling. We can use a simple rating system (such as a scale of 1-5) or write down a few words to describe our mood. No matter which method we choose, we should be consistent and track our mood regularly. Over time, we'll be able to identify patterns and triggers that affect our mental health.

It's also helpful to be aware of common triggers. For example, people, places, and things that we associate with our addiction, such as old drinking buddies or the bar where we used to hang out, can all be triggers. Similarly, stress, anxiety, and boredom are all common triggers. So, be mindful of these triggers and take steps to avoid or cope with them.

Another way to learn about triggers that we might not be aware of is to ask for feedback from others. We can ask our loved ones, therapist, or sponsor if they've noticed any patterns in our behavior or mood that might indicate a trigger. Sometimes, we're too close to our own experiences to see things objectively, so an outside perspective can be helpful.

What are some triggers others pointed out to you that you were unaware of?

___

Practicing mindfulness can be another helpful friend when it comes discovering a few of our triggers. Mindfulness can help us become more aware of our thoughts and feelings in the present moment. By paying attention to our thoughts and emotions, we may be able to identify triggers that we may not have noticed before.

Another great way to learn about our own triggers is to listen to what triggers other recovering alcoholics and addicts. Attend support group meetings to hear from others in recovery about their experiences with triggers. We may also learn new strategies for managing triggers that could work for us from others in the group as well.

What triggers have you learned you have by listening to the triggers of others?

___

Building self-awareness is like having a superpower. It helps us to recognize our triggers before they become a problem. Plus, it comes in handy during awkward social situations.

Remember, recognizing our triggers is an ongoing process and it may take a little longer than we think or would like by the time we identified all of the major ones, let alone much of the smaller ones. We may discover new triggers as we continue our recovery journey, so it's important to stay vigilant and continue to practice self-awareness.

Managing Triggers

Now, let's talk about how to manage triggers. The first thing we might want to do is make a list of our known triggers. Write down the people, places, and things that you already know trigger your addictive behavior. But be warned, this list can be longer than your Amazon shopping cart.

What triggers do you have that you already know about?

_____
_____
_____
_____
_____
_____
_____
_____
_____
_____
_____
_____
_____
_____
_____
_____

In the meanwhile, begin to identify the root cause for each trigger. I strongly encourage everyone to do this work with a professional such as a qualified counselor or therapist. If we uncover new trauma, we're gonna need an expert who knows how to deal with that shit.

Understanding the root cause of our triggers is key to managing them. It's like being a detective, but instead of a magnifying glass, we're armed with introspection and reflection.

Pick one major trigger. What do you believe is the root cause?

_____
_____
_____
_____
_____
_____
_____

Pick a second major trigger. What do you believe is the root cause?

_____
_____
_____
_____
_____
_____
_____

Pick one minor trigger. What do you believe is the root cause?

_____
_____
_____
_____
_____
_____
_____

Pick another minor trigger. What do you believe is the root cause?

_____
_____
_____
_____
_____
_____
_____

This should go without saying but let's be real. It's much easier said than done but avoid the obvious. Avoiding the people, places, and things that trigger us can be pretty difficult but if we know something is a trigger, we should avoid it like a dog avoids bath time.

Something that many of us miss the first time around in our recovery journey (and some of us miss the first dozen times) is to plan for high-risk situations. There are times where we simply cannot avoid one of these. If we know we will be in a high-risk situation, plan ahead for how we will cope with triggers. For example, if we have to attend an office party for our promotion or to do a presentation and we know that alcohol will be served, plan to bring a non-alcoholic beverage and have an escape plan in case we feel triggered.

Which brings me to this point: create a trigger plan. Write out a plan that includes a list of triggers, how you will recognize them, and what you will do to navigate them. Of course, it makes sense to actually work on making our trigger plan *after* we look at ways to manage our triggers and can have new thoughts about it that are outside the box we are currently in.

Making Trigger Plans

One approach to managing triggers is to practice what is called the "3 D's": Delay, Distract, and Decide. When we feel a craving coming on (or it hits us up the back of our head like a brick), delay acting on it for a few minutes. Then, distract ourself by doing something else, like taking a walk, calling a friend, coloring in a coloring book, or working on a project. The last one works best for me. Finally, decide what action we're going to take, whether it's to avoid the trigger altogether or to engage in a healthier activity.

Another strategy is to use positive self-talk and affirmations. When we're faced with a trigger, we need to remind ourselves of all the progress we've made in our recovery and all the reasons that we want to stay sober. We can even give ourself a little pep talk, like *"I am strong, I am capable, and I can do this!"* Bonus points if you say it in a goofy accent or squeaky voice!

If we find it difficult to talk like that to ourself, then maybe we can imagine that we are talking to a good friend but word it in the first person. If we would encourage a good friend by telling them that they are stronger than they think, then say something like *"I'm stronger than my addiction."* If we were going to support our good friend and tell them that they got this, then say, *"I got this."* And if we need more motivation, we can try adding a catchy jingle to the end of our mantra.

It could help if we create a list of positive affirmations ahead of time that we can say to ourself when we feel triggered. Examples include *"I am strong and in control,"* *"I am capable of managing this situation,"* *"I am making progress in my recovery,"* and *"I am getting better and stronger every day."* Start building this list of affirmations.

What are some self-supportive things that you can say to yourself?

_____
_____
_____
_____
_____
_____
_____

Stress is a major trigger for many people. Learning healthy ways to cope with stress can diffuse or even prevent triggers. Identify and practice coping skills that work for you, like journaling, exercising, listening to music, meditation, yoga, or binge-watching your favorite show on Netflix. These coping skills can help you manage triggers when they arise.

What coping strategies for stress do you currently use?

Do they work for you?

What would you like to try to help alleviate stress?

Adopting healthy habits can help you manage your triggers. Instead of hitting the bottle, hit the gym or take up a new hobby, like underwater basket weaving or spelunking volcanos.

What new habits would you like to work on?

One of the most important things we can do to manage our triggers is to set boundaries and stick to them. And let's face it, this has always been a very weak spot for many of us. Setting boundaries with people or situations that trigger us can help us avoid those triggers. For example, if being around certain people triggers us, we can limit our time with them or avoid them altogether.

What boundaries have you had a difficult time sticking to?

Why is that?

Do you allow others to push or disrespect your boundaries? Give examples.

Why is that?

What boundaries do you think you should have but don't?

Why haven't you put those into place yet?

Taking care of yourself (self-care) can reduce the likelihood of being triggered. Relaxation techniques such as deep breathing, progressive muscle relaxation, and meditation can also help lower your chances of being triggered. Mindfulness can help you stay present and aware of your thoughts and feelings and reduce your reactivity to triggers. It's like having a ninja sensei who teaches you how to dodge the triggers like a pro.

And don't forget to celebrate small victories. Celebrate your victories, no matter how small they may seem. Whether it's going a day without your addiction or successfully avoiding a trigger in a single moment, celebrate with a victory dance or a high five.

What does your victory dance look like anyway? You don't know how often you might have to use this, even in front others. So, for this exercise, you're going to practice a victory dance. If you don't already have one, develop one.

Do you have a victory dance? What does that look like?

_____
_____
_____
_____
_____
_____

Have you practiced your victory dance enough to feel comfortable doing it in front those you know?

_____
_____
_____
_____

What about in public, like the grocery store or mall, where you will be around complete strangers?

_____
_____
_____
_____
_____
_____

Finally, do not underestimate the importance of building a support system. Surround yourself with people who are supportive of your recovery and who will help you through difficult times. This can be friends, family members, a support group, or counselor. And don't be afraid to ask for help when you need it. After all, we all need a little help sometimes - even superheroes.

- <u>Create a support network</u>: Build a support network of friends, family, group peers at meetings, a sponsor, and other professionals who understand your struggles. These people can cheer you on during your successes and bolster you during the tough times.
- <u>Seek professional help</u>: If you are really struggling with triggers, don't be afraid to seek professional help from a qualified therapist, counselor, or addiction recovery specialist. They can help you develop coping strategies that work for you and provide support as you navigate recovery.
- <u>Identify your support system</u>: Make a list of people you can turn to when you feel triggered, such as a sponsor, therapist, friend, or family member.

Now we will work on our trigger plans. Let's include a list of triggers, how we will recognize them, and what we will do to navigate them.

For the purpose of organization, let's first make a list of our triggers. Note that there are enough slots for 30 triggers. This doesn't mean that you are expected to work with exactly 30. You might have more that you want to list so go ahead and use a notebook. But many of us might only begin with 10 or five or even just three. Whatever you do, do not overwhelm yourself with this. Remember, you *will always* come back to this, it's a discovery journey!

Great, now that we have a list to work with, let's start by looking at how we will recognize these triggers. In the shaded box, name the trigger and in the white space provided, how you will recognize it.

Once you have recognized the trigger, how will you navigate and manage it? In the shaded box, name the trigger and in the white space provided, what you will do to manage it.

Be aware that managing triggers is a process and what works for one person may not work for another. It's important to experiment with different strategies and find what works for you. It may take some trial and error to find your best tools, but you will find them with persistence, the one thing we addicts have plenty of! Before you know it, you will learn to identify and manage your triggers like a boss.

Recovery can be tough, but it's also a chance to learn, grow, and become the best version of yourself. And don't forget to keep a sense of humor throughout your journey. Recovery might be very serious business, but that doesn't mean we can't have a little fun along the way.

OH! By the way, you have made it this far which is a BIG victory. You know the drill, it's time to get up off your ass and *DO YOUR VICTORY DANCE NOW!* **You're fucking amazing!!**

Understanding Acceptance and Surrender

Understanding acceptance and surrender is a vital part of addiction recovery. Acceptance means acknowledging the reality of our situation, while surrender involves letting go of the things that are outside of our control. Both are important tools that can help us find peace and build resilience as we navigate the challenges of addiction recovery.

Acceptance

Acceptance is like opening up the window to let some fresh air into a stuffy room. It's the process of recognizing and acknowledging reality for what it is, even if it's not what we want it to be. In addiction recovery, acceptance means admitting that we have a problem, acknowledging the damage our problem has caused, and accepting that we need to make changes in order to heal ourselves and those we have hurt.

Acceptance is essential for recovery because without it, we're just spinning our wheels in the mud. If we refuse to accept the reality of our situation, we can't move forward and make progress. It's like trying to drive a car with the emergency brake on - we're not going anywhere. Acceptance allows us to let go of the past, stop fighting against what we can't change, and focus on what we can do in the present to create a better future for ourselves.

First, we need to accept the things we cannot change, like our past mistakes, the actions of others, and the inevitable ups and downs of life. We can't control everything, but we can control how we respond to it.

Next, we need to accept our feelings, even the uncomfortable ones. It's okay to feel angry, sad, anxious, or overwhelmed. Trying to push these emotions away or ignore them altogether only leads to more pain and suffering.

Third, we need to accept our limitations. We can't do everything all at once, and we can't be perfect all the time. We need to acknowledge our weaknesses and ask for help when we need it.

Finally, we need to accept ourselves as we are, flaws and all. We don't have to be perfect to be worthy of love and respect. We can work on improving self without judging or criticizing ourselves in the process.

So, acceptance is about embracing reality and allowing ourselves to feel and be who we truly are without judgment or resistance. It's a key ingredient in the recipe for a healthy and fulfilling recovery and life.

Let's begin with the Serenity Prayer. We don't have to be religious to use this as a tool for developing acceptance. Simply repeating this mantra to ourself can help us to accept the things we can't change and move on from them. Let's practice so we can remember this in times of difficulty. We can always leave out the word "God" if we wish, it will still have the same impact 😊.

"God, grant me the serenity to accept the things I cannot change, the courage to change the things I can, and the wisdom to know the difference."

Write it as many times as you can fit in the space provided and say it out loud before and after you write it out.

___
___
___
___
___
___
___
___
___
___
___
___
___
___
___
___
___
___
___
___

Next up is embracing the present moment. Many of our struggles come from dwelling on the past or worrying about the future. By embracing the present moment, we can learn to accept what's happening right now and stop ruminating on what's already happened or what might *possibly* happen in the future. One way to do this is to practice mindfulness meditation which was covered in chapter three, Mindfulness Practices.

Embracing the present moment isn't always easy, especially if it's an uncomfortable or challenging situation. But we can still embrace the present moment nonetheless and come away better people for it. Here are a few tips for embracing the present moment in uncomfortable situations:

- <u>Take a deep breath</u>: When we feel stressed or anxious, our breathing can become shallow and rapid. Taking a deep breath can help us slow down, focus on the present moment, and calm our nerves.
- <u>Practice self-compassion</u>: It's okay to feel uncomfortable or upset in challenging situations. Try to practice self-compassion by acknowledging your feelings and reminding yourself that everyone makes mistakes.
- <u>Reframe the situation</u>: Sometimes, the way we think about a situation can make it seem worse than it really is. Try to reframe the situation in a more positive or constructive light. For example, instead of thinking "*my boss is reprimanding me because she doesn't like me*," you could change that to "*my boss is giving me valuable feedback that will serve me or help me to improve.*"

Ah, reframing - the art of taking a shitty situation and slapping a new label on it to make it seem less crappy. It feels like putting a mustache on a turd and calling it a work of art.

But in all seriousness, reframing is a powerful tool for changing the way we view a situation. It's like putting on a new pair of glasses - suddenly, everything looks a little different.

So, how do we reframe an uncomfortable situation? First, we need to identify the negative thoughts and beliefs that are fueling our discomfort. Maybe we're thinking "*My boss hates me*" or "*I'm going to get fired.*" These thoughts can make us feel helpless and anxious, which only makes the situation worse.

Once we've identified these thoughts, we can start to challenge them. Is there any evidence that our boss hates us? Does the boss treat everyone in the same manner? Is it possible that the boss is just giving us accurate albeit harsh feedback to help us improve? By questioning our negative beliefs, we can start to see the situation in a new light.

Another way to reframe is to focus on the positive aspects of the situation. Maybe we can see this reprimanding as our boss giving us a chance to improve our performance or giving us an opportunity to learn a new skill. By shifting our focus to something more positive, we can start to feel more empowered and less victimized.

And finally, we can reframe by putting the situation into perspective. Is this really the end of the world? Or is it just a minor blip in the grand scheme of the universe? By taking a step back and seeing the situation in the larger context of our lives, we can start to feel more calm and centered.

Of course, reframing is easier said than done. It takes practice and patience to shift our thinking patterns. But with time, we can learn to reframe even the most uncomfortable situations and find a little bit of light in the darkness.

Think of a an uncomfortable (shitty) situation you had. What happened?

What assumptions did you make about the situation?

Are the assumptions accurate or based on your own biases and beliefs?

What are the long-term consequences of this situation?

How important is it in the grand scheme of things?

Is there another way to view the situation? What are some other perspectives that might be more helpful or empowering?

What can you learn from this? What new insights or knowledge can you gain?

How can you use this to grow and develop as a person?

How can your values and priorities help you navigate this situation, or an identical one in the future, in a more positive and productive way?

_____
_____
_____
_____
_____
_____

How can you address this in a way that aligns with your values and goals?

_____
_____
_____
_____
_____
_____

Who can you turn to for support or guidance or who can help you reframe this?

_____
_____
_____
_____

What can you learn from their perspective?

_____
_____
_____
_____
_____
_____
_____
_____

Reframing an uncomfortable situation does take practice and patience, but it can ultimately help us become more resilient and better able to handle and accept *"life on life's terms"*.

This moves us straight into the next way to help in developing acceptance, focus on the positive.

It's easy to get caught up in negative thoughts and feelings, but this only makes it harder to accept difficult situations. We should try to focus on the positive aspects of our life, no matter how small. We can keep a gratitude journal and write down a minimum of three things that we're grateful for each day. A gratitude list can help to cultivate a more positive mind-set.

Write things that you are grateful for on index cards and carry them with you. Make sure to read them three or more times a day, adding to them as more things that you feel grateful for come up. It's also important to remove anything off your list that you no longer feel grateful for. Keeping them on it could cause negative feelings including shame because you don't feel grateful for it anymore.

I'm going to ask you to list some things that you feel grateful for. I know that this is a difficult task for many of us so I will share a few of mine to help get your mental juices flowing in this positive space. I am grateful for:

Indoor plumbing   Toilet paper   Humor   Waterfalls
Warm, fuzzy socks on a cold day
I don't have to squeeze poop out of chickens for a living (Seriously, that's a job!)

Now it's your turn. What are some things that you feel grateful for:

_____ | _____
_____ | _____
_____ | _____
_____ | _____
_____ | _____
_____ | _____

Anytime we completely and utterly fail or even just make a human mistake, it's easy for us to beat ourselves up about it. But this only makes it harder to move on and accept what's happened. Instead, we should practice self-compassion by treating ourself with kindness, understanding, and support. We can start by writing ourself a compassionate letter, like we would write to a beloved friend.

AND...Oh yes! We are going to practice writing compassionate letters to ourselves! You know I had to do this! We do need to learn that we are valuable and loveable too! I personally found this exercise to be immensely valuable! It truly did contribute to the extreme shift in my self-talk. Or should I say self-abuse? Ya, for as much as I dreaded writing letters to myself, it actually turned out to be a pretty powerful tool on my road to recovery!

Alrighty then, let's grab a pen and get started. But first, we need to remember that the goal of writing these letters to ourself is to offer self-compassion, kindness, and support. We need to write with warmth and sincerity, and allow ourself to feel the emotions that arise as we write.

Write a letter to yourself from the perspective of a close friend or family member who is offering words of encouragement and support.

Think of a difficult time in your life. Write a letter to your past self, offering comfort, reassurance, and acceptance.

Write a letter to your future self, acknowledging your hopes and dreams and offering words of encouragement, support, and motivation.

Remember a mistake that you made or a time when you failed. Write a letter to yourself, acknowledging your feelings of disappointment and pain and offering forgiveness and compassion.

We all know those negative thoughts that pop into our head and try to bring us down, right? Yeah, those guys are the worst. Negative beliefs can hold us back and make it all the harder to accept difficult situations.

Oh, negative beliefs, how we love to cling to you! You make us feel shitty about ourselves and the world around us, and who doesn't love a good pity party? Negative beliefs are like those pesky house flies that won't go away no matter how many times you swat at them. But don't worry, we *can* fight back!

The thing about negative beliefs is that they're often not even based in reality, yet we hold onto them as if they're gospel truth. It's like we're wearing a pair of glasses that only allow us to see the negative aspects of ourselves and the world. Thanks, negative beliefs, for being such a faithful companion!

Negative beliefs can really hold us back in life. They make it difficult to take risks, try new things, and step outside of our comfort zones. All things that we need in order to grow as humans. So, it's important to challenge them and see them for what they are - just thoughts, *not facts*.

Let's take some time to reflect on a few of our negative beliefs and challenge them. We want to ask ourself if they're really true and what evidence is there to support those beliefs. Then, we want to look for evidence that contradicts them. We might be surprised at what we find.

Write a few of your negative beliefs then write a counterargument for each one.

Negative Belief:	Counter argument:
Negative Belief:	Counter argument:
Negative Belief:	Counter argument:

Sometimes, we have to breakdown a negative belief because it really has more than one belief built in. For example: *"I am a fat lazy pig."* Here we have several beliefs. *"I am fat," "I am lazy,"* and *"I am a pig."* Perhaps we have evidence that we are overweight. Did the doctor tell us that? That would be evidence. But what about the rest of those beliefs that stem from the one?

Where is the evidence that we are a pig? Do we have a long snout? Are we pink? Do we have a corkscrew tail? If you answered yes to *all* of these, then you might be a redneck. Oh, I mean we might be a *pig*. But if we answered no to just one of those questions, then we are indeed *not* a pig!

Make a short list of some of your negative beliefs. Highlight any that may have more than one built in.

___

Now, rewrite the ones that have more than one built in and break them down into their individual beliefs.

Negative Belief:	The Individual Breakdown:
Negative Belief:	The Individual Breakdown:
Negative Belief:	The Individual Breakdown:

Let's challenge our negative thoughts or beliefs and try to find evidence that contradicts them. And remember, negative thoughts are just that, *thoughts* - they don't define who we are. We are worthy and deserving of love, happiness, and respect no matter what our negative thoughts might tell us.

When we catch ourselves thinking something negative, we need to step back and really examine it. Is that negative thought really true? Are there any other ways to see the situation that might be more positive? And most importantly, is that negative thought really helping us in any way? Probably not.

Negative thought/belief	True?	Serves me?	Positive way to look at it
Negative thought/belief	True?	Serves me?	Positive way to look at it
Negative thought/belief	True?	Serves me?	Positive way to look at it
Negative thought/belief	True?	Serves me?	Positive way to look at it

Remember, developing acceptance takes time and practice. Be patient with yourself and keep working at it, and you'll start to see progress over time.

Surrender

Ah, surrender, the act of throwing in the towel and giving up. Sounds like a real winner, right? I mean, just the sound of it makes us want to throw our hands in the air and completely give up. Well, in a way, that's kind of what it is. Surrender is about letting go of control and allowing things to unfold as they will.

Surrender might seem counterintuitive but it's an essential part of recovery, despite what our ego might tell us. And why is it essential for recovery? Because sometimes trying to control everything is what got us into this fucked up mess in the first place.

When we surrender, we're not giving up, we're just acknowledging that there are some things that are beyond our control. It's about learning to be okay with uncertainty and finding peace in the midst of chaos. And let's face it, life is chaotic, so we might as well find a way to get comfortable with it.

But don't worry, surrender doesn't mean giving up all responsibility for your life. It just means learning to let go of the things you can't control and focusing your energy on the things you can. It's about finding a balance between effort and ease, action and acceptance.

So, if we want to recover, we'd better get comfortable with surrender. But how can we put surrender into practice? Well, first, we have to be willing to let go of the need to control everything. Yes, that's right, we're not the masters of the universe (shocking, I know).

Next, we should try to be open to the possibility that things might not always go our way. I know, I know, this might be hard to accept, but trust me, it's for the best. Remember, we're not the center of the universe, and sometimes things happen that are out of our control.

Another way to practice surrender is to let go of our attachment to outcomes. Instead of focusing on the end result, try to enjoy the journey and be present in the moment. After all, life is all about the journey, not just the destination.

And finally, try to embrace the unknown. Surrendering means accepting that there are things in life that we just don't know or understand, and that's okay. Instead of fighting it, let's try to embrace the mystery and see where it takes us.

Developing surrender is all about letting go of control and learning to go with the flow. Like a leaf floating down a river or a bird soaring through the sky. And I know, it's not always that easy.

One way to develop surrender is to practice letting go of the things that are outside of our control. We can start by identifying the things that we have no control over and acknowledging that we can't change them. For example, we can't control the weather, traffic, or other people's behavior. Once we've identified these things, we can practice accepting them as they are and letting go of any frustration or stress that they might be causing us.

List some things that are *NOT* in your control:

_____

_____

_____

_____

_____

_____

Another way to develop surrender is to practice mindfulness and being present in the moment. Isn't mindfulness getting to be a pattern here? In particular here, we focus on what's happening in the moment instead of worrying about the future or dwelling on the past. Mindfulness can help us let go of the need to control everything and simply be present in the moment.

We can also try practicing gratitude and appreciation. By focusing on the things that we're thankful for, we can cultivate a sense of acceptance and surrender. Keep working with the gratitude index cards you started earlier three times a day or more.

Developing surrender takes time and practice. It's not something that will happen overnight, so we need to be patient with ourselves and keep at it. And if all else fails, just remember the wise words of Elsa from Frozen: "*Let it go, let it go!*"

List things that you're struggling to control even though you can't control them. This could include relationships, work, finances, health, behavior or beliefs of others, etc. Take a moment to acknowledge that these are beyond your control.

_____
_____
_____
_____
_____
_____
_____
_____
_____
_____

Embrace the uncertainty of life. Life is unpredictable and full of unknowns. Instead of trying to control everything, learn to accept the uncertainty and trust that everything will work out in the end.

List your worries about the future, no matter how big or small they may be. Now, challenge each one by asking yourself if it is a realistic worry and whether it is something you can control.

Worry for the Future	Realistic?	Can I Control it?

Make a list of times when things worked out well for you, even, and especially, if you were unsure of the outcome at the time. Use this list to remind yourself that you have a history of success and things will likely work out in the end.

_____
_____
_____
_____
_____
_____
_____
_____
_____
_____
_____
_____
_____
_____

Let's take some time to visualize a positive outcome for a situation that we are uncertain about. Imagine everything working out well and how we will feel once it does. The more detail we give our visualization, the better. This can help us to develop a more positive outlook and trust in the outcome.

What did you visualize?

_____
_____
_____
_____
_____
_____
_____
_____
_____

How did it feel during the visualization?

_____
_____
_____
_____
_____
_____
_____
_____
_____
_____
_____
_____
_____

How did it feel after?

_____
_____
_____
_____
_____
_____
_____
_____
_____
_____
_____
_____
_____

    Each time we successfully face an uncertain situation, we build up our confidence and trust in ourself and the future. With this in mind, practice taking small steps towards uncertainty. Let's do a few new or challenging things that we have been nervous about and avoiding. Start out small, we don't want to get inundated which will just push us further away from facing these things.

What did you do?

How did they work out?

How do you feel about them now?

Often, our struggles with surrender come from our expectations of how things should be. We press our personal list of should's on everyone and everything in our world but the reality is that everyone has their own journey to walk. And no two look the same. Nor should they. Practice letting go of these expectations and accepting things and people as they are. Look, we want others to respect our beliefs and our life's journey so we ought to practice the same respect in return.

So you see, surrender is not about giving up or giving in. It's about acknowledging that there are things beyond our control and learning to let go of the struggle. By developing surrender, we can find peace and freedom in the midst of some very difficult situations.

Just remember that, *it is what it is and nothing more!* Oh, that sounds great! Let's practice this so we can remember it in times of power struggle.

"It is what it is, and nothing more."

Write the above statement as many times as you can fit in the space provided and say it out loud before and after you write it out.

So, here's the deal: acceptance and surrender are like two peas in a pod. They go together like peanut butter and jelly, wine and cheese, peas and carrots, or twinkies and chocolate sauce. And just like the aforementioned pairs, you can have one without the other, but they're oh so much better together!

Acceptance is all about recognizing what is, without trying to change it or fight against it. Surrender, on the other hand, is about letting go of the need to control everything and trusting that things will somehow work out in the end.

When we combine acceptance and surrender, we create a powerful force that can help us navigate even the toughest situations. We're no longer fighting against reality or trying to force things to be a certain way. Instead, we're open to what is and willing to trust that things will work out in the end, even if we don't know how. This, my friends, is living *"life on life's terms!"*

The benefits of acceptance and surrender are many. We'll experience greater peace and calm, because we're no longer resisting what is. We'll be able to let go of stress and anxiety, because we're not constantly trying to control things. And we'll be more present in the moment, because we're not lost in our worries about the future or regrets about the past.

So, if we want to find greater peace, calm, and happiness in our life, all we need do is practice acceptance and surrender. They may not be the most intuitive or easy things to do, but they are most certainly worth it!

It's time for another *VICTORY DANCE NOW!*
You're smashing this shit!!

Forgiveness and Making Amends

Oh, forgiveness and making amends. Two classic elements of the addiction recovery journey and what a lovely topic! I mean, who doesn't love apologizing to assholes and making things right?

Ya, the dreaded F-word: forgiveness. It's not exactly a fun or sexy topic, but it's an important one for anyone in the addiction recovery game. And let's not forget about making amends - nothing says "I'm sorry" like a heartfelt apology with a change in behavior or some good old-fashioned restitution.

We all know that forgiving and making amends can be some of the hardest things to do, especially when we've been hurt or wronged by others (or worse, when we were the ones doing the wrongs or hurting).

So why bother with all of this? Well, aside from the fact that holding grudges and harboring guilt – including that which we are unaware of – can seriously mess with our mental health, it's also pretty hard to move forward and create a happy, fulfilling life when we're bogged down by all that emotional baggage.

But hey, that's why we're here, right? To work on being better versions of ourselves and learning to forgive and make things right when we fuck up, regardless of whether others have any blame. It's for us to mind our own p's and q's. Now, let's dive into these topics, shall we?

Forgiveness

First up, forgiveness. The ultimate act of letting go, right? It's like taking all that anger, hurt, and resentment that we've been holding onto and saying, "*You know what? I'm over it.*" Of course, it's far easier said than done.

But why is forgiveness so important in the recovery process? Well, holding onto grudges and resentments can be incredibly draining and super toxic to our mental and emotional well-being. It's like carrying around a heavy weight that just keeps dragging us down. But by forgiving those who have wronged us, we're actually releasing that weight and allowing ourself to move on and heal.

Plus, forgiveness isn't about the other person anyway. It's about ourself. When we hold onto anger and resentment, it can consume us and affect our relationships with others. But when we choose to forgive, we're making a conscious decision to let go of those negative emotions and create space for more positivity and joy in our life.

Now let's be clear on something right here and now. Forgiveness is NOT about letting the other person or people off the hook. Nor does it mean that we have to continue to allow someone in our life and in a capacity to be able to continue to wrong us in the same ways. Sometimes, forgiving someone includes kicking them OUT of our life, for the sake of our good health.

Forgiveness is about finding peace within ourself, regardless of the other person's actions and whether or not they remain in our life.

It's not always easy to forgive, especially when someone has wronged us in a big way. But forgiveness is not about letting the other person off the hook, it's about releasing ourselves from the burden and negative energy of anger and resentment. So, how do we practice forgiveness?

We can start by acknowledging all the pain, hurt, or anger that we have experienced. It's important to feel our feelings and not just brush them under the rug. Recognize that forgiveness is a process, not a one-time event. It may take time and effort to work through our emotions and come to a place of peaceful forgiveness.

Sometimes we get hurt or feel like we have been wronged when the other person is actually completely innocent. Perhaps they were in an extremely difficult situation themselves or there was a piece of information they didn't have. For this reason, we also practice empathy and understanding. We try to put ourself in the other person's shoes and see things from their perspective.

A technique that I use is asking the universe to send that person a blessing. I know this sounds weird but hear me out. First of all, I have to be able to get behind the blessing that I am asking my higher power to send. It has to fit the situation and I have to mean it. Until I do this, I have no peace, no matter how many times I *say* that I forgive the person.

If someone lied to me, I will ask my God to bless that person with the truth, because if they had the truth, they would know that they would never have to lie. Nor would they if they had the truth!

If someone caused a lot of turmoil in my life, I might ask the universe to send them peace. If they had peace, they would have no need for drama. I asked to send a narcissist real love because I believed that if he had that, then he wouldn't hurt anyone else. And for someone who has trouble keeping his word, I asked my God to straighten his feet out so he could do the right thing.

This little trick releases me faster than anything else. I usually have to sit and really think for a while about what blessing (or positive energy) I want the universe to send the other person. B.T. Dubs, I don't tell the other person that I sent them a blessing lest they think they can do whatever it was again. Remember, the forgiveness was never about them, it was always about me and my peace.

Even if we don't pray, we could still use this technique, simply change the praying part with sending the specific positive energy to the other person, like sending them the energy of truth.

Your turn. List someone that hurt or angered you then think of some positive energy that you can feel good about sending their way.

Who Upset Me:	Blessing/Positive Energy to Send:

Writing a letter can be pretty powerful too. This is one I used to use and was quite effective. I always called these letters "Dear John" letters, no matter the relationship I had with the person. I called them that because I was at a point of not allowing the person to wrong me. Sometimes it meant moving them out of my life and other times it meant moving them into a different position. One where they could no longer affect me in whatever negative way. For instance, moving someone I had considered a good friend to an acquaintance level.

Most times, the letter I wrote never got sent. Of course, when I began the letter, I had the intention to send it, letting them know what an asshole they are. I wrote countless letters that never got sent but rather were put into my personal notebook. I kept letters like that to remind myself that this was not a person to trust in that particular capacity again, lest I fall back into denial.

But let's be honest here, if someone told us that we should send a letter of "forgiveness" to someone that wronged us or hurt us, this would surely piss us off! But listen Linda, listen! We don't have to start writing that letter in a loving tone.

When I would sit down to write a "forgiveness" letter, it would start out pretty harsh with quite colorful language, pointing out to said person what they had done and why it was so shitty. I would have all kinds of projection shit in the beginning of the letter. I would just let my pen flow with my emotions, pointing out everything. Eventually, I would calm down and that's when I would begin to see things in a different light and sometimes even from the other side (when possible).

Ultimately, the tone of the letter would turn assertive and maybe even kind of tender. I would view things from the other person's perspective. This is when I would be able to forgive the person and state how the relationship was going to change. "*This is why I can no longer keep you in an important capacity in my life.*" Or, "*For my mental and emotional wellbeing, I can no longer allow you in my life."* From there, I would honestly wish them well on their life journey. Why? Because I forgave them and what happened and moved on.

Try writing a forgiveness letter, even if you never send it. This can be a powerful way to release your emotions and work through the process of forgiveness so you can finally be set free from the hurt, anger, and feelings of betrayal.

Now, let's talk about forgiving the most important person in our life. Ourself. We can be so shitty to ourselves! If we were to do to someone else some of the shit we have done to ourselves, we'd probably get locked up. But for some reason, this garbage is acceptable when it comes to one's self. Isn't this ass-backwards? Dysfunction at its finest!

How can we expect others to treat us with respect when we don't treat ourselves with respect. We are the example to the world how we should be treated. And that, boys and girls, begins with how we treat ourselves. If we keep someone in our life that repeatedly disrespects or hurts us in some way, we show the world that it is acceptable and even expected for everyone to disrespect us. This is a show to the world that we believe that we have little to no value as a person.

We have fucked ourselves over many, many times. We have proven to ourselves that we cannot be trusted with our own wellbeing be it mental, emotional, financial, physical, psychological, or spiritual. It's time to STOP! We need to let go of the pain we have caused ourselves so we can clear our space, find self-trust, and move forward with a little peace. We need to forgive ourselves.

Writing letters to forgive ourselves can be a helpful and cathartic exercise. Often, we are much harder on ourselves than we would ever be on someone else, and we hold onto guilt and shame long after we should have let it go. By writing a forgiveness letter to ourselves, we are acknowledging that we are human, that we make mistakes, and that *we are worthy of love and forgiveness.*

The letters can help guide us through the process of self-forgiveness and allow us to explore our feelings and emotions in a safe and structured way. They can also help us identify patterns of negative self-talk and self-sabotage, and work through them in a compassionate and healing way.

Ultimately, self-forgiveness is a powerful tool for healing and personal growth, and writing a forgiveness letter to ourselves can be an effective step in that process.

Let's start with writing a letter forgiving ourself for becoming an addict.

Moving on. Let's write a letter forgiving ourself for not protecting ourselves and allowing others to hurt us.

Now, let's write a letter of forgiveness for the pain that we have caused ourself through our negative self-talk and destructive behavior.

Making Amends

Now, let's dive into making amends, shall we?

First, let's define exactly what we mean by *making amends*. Essentially, making amends involves acknowledging and taking responsibility for our past actions that have harmed others and actively working to repair the harm we've caused in order to make things right. It's a key part of the recovery process, particularly for those struggling with other destructive behaviors. Making amends can help repair damaged relationships and provide a sense of closure, both for the person making the amends and for the people they have harmed.

Now, some people might think that making amends is just a bunch of touchy-feely bullshit, but it's actually a pretty badass thing to do. Why? Because it takes guts to own up to our garbage and face the people we've wronged. It's not easy to admit we were wrong and that we have hurt someone we care about or someone who was innocent, and it's even harder to make things right. But that's exactly what making amends is all about.

Making amends is important for a few reasons. For one, it can help to alleviate the guilt and shame that often come with addictive or destructive behaviors. When we make amends, we are acknowledging the harm we've caused and taking steps to address it. This can be a powerful way to move past our feelings of guilt and shame and start to rebuild our self-esteem and sense of self-worth.

Of course, making amends isn't just about making ourselves feel better. It's also about repairing the harm we've caused to others and the damaged relationships left in our wake due to our addictive behavior. When we hurt someone, we create a wound that can fester and grow if left unaddressed. Making amends is like applying a healing balm to that wound. It won't erase the pain, but it can help the healing process begin.

When we take responsibility for our actions and actively work to make things right, we are demonstrating our commitment to changing and improving as a person. This can be a powerful way to rebuild trust and repair relationships that may have been damaged by our behavior.

So, how do we make amends? Well, it's not a one-size-fits-all process. The specifics will depend on the situation, the people involved, and our own personal style. But in general, making amends involves a few key steps:

- <u>Acknowledge our mistake</u>. This means admitting that we fucked up, and taking responsibility for our actions.
- <u>Apologize</u>. This means saying we're sorry for what we did, and expressing *genuine* remorse.
- <u>Make things right in any way we can</u>. This might involve making restitution, offering to help in some way, doing something to show that we're committed to making things better, or simply acknowledging the harm we've caused.

Making amends isn't always easy. In fact, it can be downright uncomfortable and awkward. But if we're serious about our recovery, it's something we need to do. And who knows? We might even find that the act of making amends helps us grow and become a better, more compassionate person thus increase our attractiveness.

Making amends might not be the most glamorous part of the recovery process, but it's definitely one of the most important. It takes guts, it takes heart, and it takes a willingness to face our own flaws and shortcomings.

We're going to make a list of people we have harmed. This can be a difficult exercise, but it's an important first step in the process of making amends. Let's take some time to reflect on our past behavior and think about the people we may have hurt along the way.

In the shaded box, write the names of 10 people you hurt and in the white space provided, how you have harmed them. (You will be speaking to at least two of them soon to make your amends.)

Who I Harmed	What I Did or Said

Now that we have a list of people we have harmed, we will write a letter of amends to five of them. In our letters, we want to be specific about the harm we caused and take responsibility for our actions. Let's avoid making excuses, justifications, or shifting blame onto someone else. Instead, let's just focus on acknowledging the harm *we* caused and expressing our sincere regret.

We have to be specific. We can't just say, *"I'm sorry for hurting you"*. That's not an apology. A real apology looks more like this:

"I am sorry for lying to you about xxx. You must have felt betrayed. Not only was that disrespecting you, but it was a hurtful and selfish thing for me to do. I know that I would have felt hurt and betrayed if the tables were turned. In the future, I will xxx."

Now that's an apology! A real apology will acknowledge the specific thing we did or said (*lying to you about xxx*), recognize the damage it caused (*You must have felt...*), relay why it was wrong (*disrespectful, hurtful, selfish*), how we would have felt if they did that to us (*I would have felt...*), and finally what we will do in the future instead (*In the future, I will xxx*). This is fully acknowledging what we did, the harm it caused, as well as taking responsibility for our actions by explaining how we will change our behavior in the future.

This apology shows real thought went into what we did and how it affected the other person as well as acknowledging that our behavior towards that person needs to change. Simply saying, *"I'm sorry"* is the same thing as saying, *"get over it already so I can feel better about myself."* That makes the apology about the one giving it but a real apology should be about the other person.

Write a letter of amends to one person (highlight the person in your list):

_____
_____
_____
_____
_____
_____
_____
_____
_____
_____
_____
_____
_____
_____
_____
_____
_____
_____
_____
_____

Write a letter of amends to a second person (highlight the person in your list):

Write a letter of amends to a third person (highlight the person in your list):

Write a letter of amends to a fourth person (highlight the person in your list):

Write a letter of amends to a fifth person (highlight the person in your list):

Practice active listening. When we have the opportunity to speak with the people you have harmed, we have to practice active listening. This means giving them our full attention and really hearing what they have to say. We need to avoid becoming defensive or dismissive, even if their feedback is difficult to hear. Remember, the goal of making amends is to demonstrate our commitment to changing our behavior and thereby repair relationships.

Being real, the only way we can listen to the other person is if we verbally apologize to them. So, we are going to have to step far outside of our comfort zone and approach someone we have wronged and acknowledge our wrong doing. Let's make sure we are actively listening to the other person.

After attempting a verbal amends with the first person, what did they say?

_____
_____
_____
_____
_____
_____
_____

After attempting a verbal amends with the second person, what did they say?

_____
_____
_____
_____
_____
_____
_____

When making amends, it's important to follow through on any commitments we make. If we said that we will change our behavior, make it a point do so. If we owe someone money, make arrangements to pay them back. Demonstrating that we are serious about making things right is key to rebuilding trust and repairing relationships.

It's important to take responsibility for our actions and make things right. Remember that a real amends is a changed behavior and our behavior, boys and girls, is a choice!

Finally, be patient and respectful of the other person's process. They may not be ready to forgive or accept our amends right away, and that's okay. Just keep showing up with sincerity and a willingness to make things right, allowing them to take as long as they need.

Well, I don't know about you, but I found this chapter to be emotionally challenging. Feel free to get up and do your VICTORY DANCE NOW! **You're fucking badass!!**

Summary & Resources:

Well, well, well, look at us now! My but haven't we grown so big, so fast! We've covered a lot of ground in *The Brave Guide* and we're feeling pretty fuckin' good about ourselves, aren't we? And so we should! We've learned about and begun practicing self-care, mindfulness, managing our triggers, acceptance, surrender, forgiveness, and making amends. That's a lot of heavy lifting and we deserve a pat on the back for sticking with it! **You're fucking amazing!**

We've discussed how important it is to prioritize our physical and mental health in order to support our recovery journey. We explored a range of self-care practices, including exercise, healthy eating, and getting enough sleep. We also discussed the importance of support from others.

Then there was mindfulness. We talked about how mindfulness practices can help us become more present in the moment and develop greater awareness of our thoughts, feelings, and behaviors. We explored different mindfulness techniques, such as guided meditation, body scan, and breathing exercises.

We also delved into identifying and managing our triggers. We discussed how triggers can be anything that sets off a chain reaction of thoughts, emotions, and behaviors that can lead to a slip or relapse. We explored strategies for identifying triggers, such as keeping a trigger tracker journal, and discussed ways to manage them, like using new coping skills, and avoiding high-risk situations.

Acceptance and surrender were also covered. We talked about the importance of accepting our circumstances, including the fact that we have an addiction. We explored how surrendering can help us let go of our need for control and find greater peace and serenity.

Finally, we delved into the topics of forgiveness and making amends. We discussed how holding onto resentments and grudges can be a major obstacle to recovery, and explored how forgiveness can help us move forward. We also talked about the importance of making amends to those we have harmed, and discussed strategies for doing so.

But wait, there's more! We can't stop now, oh no. We need to keep using these concepts and tools, day in and day out, in order to continue our journey of recovery. It's like lifting weights - you can't just do it once and expect to see results. We need to keep at it, even and especially on the days when we don't feel like it, because that's when it really counts.

And the one thing that I know for sure is that we *can* be successful in this. We may stumble and fall along the way, but we can get back up, dust ourselves off, and keep moving forward. We have the power within us to overcome our addiction, and with the help of *The Brave Guide* and our support network, we can do it. So, let's keep at it, let's keep using these concepts, and let's keep believing in ourselves.

Remember, recovery is a journey, not a destination. But with the right tools, support, and mindset, we can continue to grow, heal, and thrive. So, keep on keepin' on bitches, *WE FUCKIN' GOT THIS!*

VICTORY DANCE TIME!!

Rounding Out Our Recovery Program

A well-rounded addiction recovery program can involve a combination of different approaches including peer support groups, group counseling, individual therapy, medication-assisted treatment when appropriate, and educational resources. The specific treatment plan will vary depending on your personal unique needs and circumstances. Be sure to work with trained, sober professionals who can help guide you in developing the most effective treatment plan for your unique needs and that will work best for your personal recovery journey.

Peer Group Support Communities

These groups offer a supportive community where members can share their experiences and struggles with addiction, learn from each other, and provide mutual support. These groups are often free to attend and are open to anyone who is seeking help with addiction recovery.

- **12 Step Recovery Fellowships** such as Alcoholics Anonymous (AA), Narcotics Anonymous (NA), and other 12 Step Programs of recovery are great for connecting with others who understand what you're going through and can offer advice and support. While most offer online and in-person support meetings, I would strongly encourage you to attend in person meetings whenever feasible.
- **S.M.A.R.T. Recovery** provides support through a science-based, self-empowering approach. The program is based on the principles of cognitive-behavioral therapy and focuses on developing skills and strategies to manage addictive behaviors. S.M.A.R.T. Recovery also offers online and in-person support meetings, as well as a variety of resources and tools for individuals in recovery. Again, I would encourage you to attend in person meetings whenever possible.

- **Refuge Recovery** uses Buddhist principles and practices to support recovery from addiction.
- **LifeRing Secular Recovery** is based on the idea that individuals have the power to overcome addiction through their own resources and motivation.
- **Women for Sobriety** is specifically designed for women in recovery and emphasizes self-help, empowerment, and personal responsibility.
- **Secular Organizations for Sobriety (SOS)** emphasizes self-empowerment, personal responsibility, and individual autonomy in recovery.
- **Moderation Management** is aimed at individuals who want to moderate their alcohol consumption rather than abstaining completely.

Not all of these programs will work for everyone so do your research and explore different options to find the program that works best for you.

Group Counseling

Group counseling is a type of therapy that involves one or more trained addiction counselors or therapists working with several people at the same time. It can be an effective form of treatment for addiction as group therapy can help people develop new coping strategies, improve communication and social skills, and build a sense of community and accountability. And it's also a great place for educational resources.

Group counseling also allows those struggling with addiction to connect with others who are going through similar struggles and share their experiences, thoughts, and feelings in a supportive and non-judgmental environment. It can be used in combination with other forms of therapy, such as peer groups as mentioned above, individual therapy, or medication-assisted treatment.

Individual Therapy

Individual therapy involves one-on-one sessions with a trained therapist. It provides a safe and nonjudgmental space for exploring your thoughts and feelings, and can help you develop coping strategies for difficult situations not to mention discover underlying causes for your behavior.

During these sessions, the therapist will work with the individual to explore their thoughts, feelings, and behaviors related to their addiction, as well as any underlying mental health issues that may be contributing to their addiction.

Individual therapy can be especially helpful for those who may not feel comfortable sharing their experiences in a group setting, or who have unique challenges or circumstances that require more personalized attention. It can also be an effective tool for addressing issues related to trauma, grief, anxiety, depression, and other co-occurring issues that often accompany addiction.

The therapist will typically use evidence-based therapies such as cognitive-behavioral therapy (CBT), dialectical behavior therapy (DBT), or motivational interviewing (MI) to help the individual gain insight into their addiction and develop new coping skills and strategies for managing triggers and cravings. The therapist may also work with the person to develop a relapse prevention plan and set goals for their recovery.

Overall, individual therapy can be a valuable component of a comprehensive treatment program for alcoholism and addiction recovery. It can provide a safe and supportive space for those struggling with addiction to explore their challenges, receive guidance and support, and develop the tools they need to achieve and maintain lasting recovery.

Medication-Assisted Treatment (MAT)

Medication-assisted treatment (MAT) is a type of treatment for addiction that uses medications to help manage withdrawal symptoms and cravings, and to reduce the risk of relapse. MAT is typically used in combination with behavioral therapies and counseling to provide a comprehensive approach to addiction treatment.

MAT can be helpful in the treatment of alcoholism for some people. MAT involves the use of medication, in combination with counseling and other behavioral therapies, to help people reduce or stop their alcohol consumption.

Acamprosate can help to reduce cravings and withdrawal symptoms, and is often used in combination with behavioral therapies. Disulfiram can help to deter alcohol use by causing unpleasant side effects when alcohol is consumed. Naltrexone can block the effects of alcohol.

The medications used in MAT for alcoholism include:

- **Naltrexone** helps reduce alcohol cravings and the pleasurable effects of drinking. It can be taken in pill form or as a monthly injection.
- **Acamprosate** helps to reduce alcohol cravings and can help people maintain abstinence from alcohol. It is taken in pill form.
- **Disulfiram** is a medication that causes unpleasant side effects when alcohol is consumed. This medication can help people stay motivated to remain abstinent.

Note that medication alone is not a cure for alcoholism or other addictions. MAT should be used in conjunction with counseling and other support to achieve the best outcomes. MAT is not appropriate for everyone, and the decision to use medication for addiction of any kind should be made in consultation with a qualified healthcare provider.

MAT can be used to treat addiction to opioids like heroin and prescription painkillers. There are several medications that are commonly used in MAT for opioid addiction, including methadone, buprenorphine, and naltrexone.

- **Methadone** is a long-acting opioid medication that can help to reduce withdrawal symptoms and cravings for opioids. It is typically dispensed at specialized clinics under close medical supervision.
- **Buprenorphine** is a partial opioid agonist that can help to reduce withdrawal symptoms and cravings, and is often prescribed by qualified healthcare providers in an office-based setting.
- **Naltrexone** is a medication that blocks the effects of opioids and can help to prevent relapse, and is often used after a person has completed detoxification.

MAT should always be used in combination with other forms of treatment, such as counseling and support groups, to provide the best chance for recovery. Again, the decision to use MAT should be made in consultation with a qualified healthcare provider and should always be overseen by a qualified healthcare provider.

MAT is also available for smoking and tobacco addiction.

- **Nicotine replacement therapy (NRT)** is considered a form of MAT for tobacco addiction. NRT products such as nicotine gum, patches, lozenges, inhalers, and nasal sprays all provide nicotine in a controlled manner to help manage withdrawal symptoms and cravings, while gradually weaning the individual off nicotine over time.
- **Bupropion** is an antidepressant that is also used to help people quit smoking. It works by reducing nicotine cravings and withdrawal symptoms. Bupropion is taken orally and is usually started a week or two before the person plans to quit smoking. Treatment with bupropion typically lasts for 7 to 12 weeks.
- **Varenicline** is a prescription medication that is specifically designed to help people quit smoking. It works by reducing the pleasurable effects of nicotine and reducing cravings for cigarettes. Varenicline is taken orally and is usually started a week or two before the person plans to quit smoking. Treatment with varenicline typically lasts for 12 weeks.

NRT, bupropion, and varenicline are all more effective when used in combination with behavioral therapy and support groups. Note that medication-assisted treatment for smoking and tobacco addiction is not recommended for everyone, and should be discussed with a qualified healthcare provider to determine if it is a suitable option for you.

Useful and Trusted Websites

For the United States

- **National Institute on Drug Abuse** (NIDA) is a government organization that provides research-based information on drug abuse and addiction. It offers resources for people seeking treatment and support, as well as resources for healthcare providers. https://www.drugabuse.gov/
- **Substance Abuse and Mental Health Services Administration** (SAMHSA) is a government agency that provides resources and information on substance abuse and mental health. It offers a national helpline for people seeking help with addiction and mental health issues.
https://www.samhsa.gov/
- **National Institute on Alcohol Abuse and Alcoholism** (NIAAA)
https://www.niaaa.nih.gov/

For the United Kingdom,

- **The national Health Service** (NHS) website has information on addiction and mental health services, as well as support groups and charities. You can also contact the NHS 111 service for urgent medical help and advice, or call the Samaritans helpline for emotional support.
https://www.nhs.uk/live-well/healthy-body/drug-addiction-getting-help/
- **Alcohol Change**: https://alcoholchange.org.uk/

For Canada

The Government of Canada's website has information on addiction and mental health services, as well as support groups and other organizations.

The Crisis Services Canada hotline helps with immediate crisis support and **Canadian Mental Health Association** offers mental health resources and support.

- **Canadian Centre on Substance Use and Addiction** (CCSA): https://www.ccsa.ca/
- **Public Health Agency of Canada** (PHAC): https://www.canada.ca/en/public-health.html

For Australia

- **Australian Government - Department of Health** provides a wide range of resources for people with addiction, including information on treatment, support, and education.
https://www.health.gov.au/health-topics/drugs/about-drugs/drug-addiction
- **Australian Drug Foundation** provides information and resources on drug and alcohol addiction, including fact sheets, online courses, and support services. https://adf.org.au/
- **Alcohol and Drug Foundation** is a national organization that provides information and resources on alcohol and drug addiction. They offer a range of support services, including online tools and resources, peer support, and telephone counselling. https://adf.org.au/help-support/
- **Counselling Online** is a free online service that provides professional support to people affected by alcohol and drug addiction. They offer online counselling, email support, and a 24/7 chat service. https://www.counsellingonline.org.au/

For Germany

- **Deutsche Hauptstelle für Suchtfragen e.V.** (DHS) is the German Federal Centre for Health Education. They provide resources and support for addiction recovery, including information on substance abuse, prevention, and treatment. Their website is available in both German and English. https://www.dhs.de/en.html
- **Die Deutsche Gesellschaft für Suchtforschung und Suchttherapie** (DG-Sucht) is a scientific organization focused on addiction research and treatment. They offer information on addiction research and treatment in Germany, including publications and events. Their website is available in German and English. https://www.dg-sucht.de/

Trigger Tracker

Date: _____ Time: _____ Place: _____
What triggered me? _____
Knee-jerk reaction: _____
Physical sensation: _____
I thought: _____
I felt: _____
Why this triggered me: _____

Date: _____ Time: _____ Place: _____
What triggered me? _____
Knee-jerk reaction: _____
Physical sensation: _____
I thought: _____
I felt: _____
Why this triggered me: _____

Date: _____ Time: _____ Place: _____
What triggered me? _____
Knee-jerk reaction: _____
Physical sensation: _____
I thought: _____
I felt: _____
Why this triggered me: _____

Date: _____ Time: _____ Place: _____
What triggered me? _____
Knee-jerk reaction: _____
Physical sensation: _____
I thought: _____
I felt: _____
Why this triggered me: _____

Date: _____ Time: _____ Place: _____
What triggered me? _____
Knee-jerk reaction: _____
Physical sensation: _____
I thought: _____
I felt: _____
Why this triggered me: _____

Date: _____ Time: _____ Place: _____
What triggered me? _____
Knee-jerk reaction: _____
Physical sensation: _____
I thought: _____
I felt: _____
Why this triggered me: _____

Date: _____ Time: _____ Place: _____
What triggered me? _____
Knee-jerk reaction: _____
Physical sensation: _____
I thought: _____
I felt: _____
Why this triggered me: _____

Date: _____ Time: _____ Place: _____
What triggered me? _____
Knee-jerk reaction: _____
Physical sensation: _____
I thought: _____
I felt: _____
Why this triggered me: _____

Date: _____ Time: _____ Place: _____
What triggered me? _____
Knee-jerk reaction: _____
Physical sensation: _____
I thought: _____
I felt: _____
Why this triggered me: _____

Date: _____ Time: _____ Place: _____
What triggered me? _____
Knee-jerk reaction: _____
Physical sensation: _____
I thought: _____
I felt: _____
Why this triggered me: _____

Date: _____ Time: _____ Place: _____
What triggered me? _____
Knee-jerk reaction: _____
Physical sensation: _____
I thought: _____
I felt: _____
Why this triggered me: _____

Date: _____ Time: _____ Place: _____
What triggered me? _____
Knee-jerk reaction: _____
Physical sensation: _____
I thought: _____
I felt: _____
Why this triggered me: _____

Date: _____ Time: _____ Place: _____
What triggered me? _____
Knee-jerk reaction: _____
Physical sensation: _____
I thought: _____
I felt: _____
Why this triggered me: _____

Date: _____ Time: _____ Place: _____
What triggered me? _____
Knee-jerk reaction: _____
Physical sensation: _____
I thought: _____
I felt: _____
Why this triggered me: _____

Date: _____ Time: _____ Place: _____
What triggered me? _____
Knee-jerk reaction: _____
Physical sensation: _____
I thought: _____
I felt: _____
Why this triggered me: _____

Date: _____ Time: _____ Place: _____
What triggered me? _____
Knee-jerk reaction: _____
Physical sensation: _____
I thought: _____
I felt: _____
Why this triggered me: _____

Date: _____ Time: _____ Place: _____
What triggered me? _____
Knee-jerk reaction: _____
Physical sensation: _____
I thought: _____
I felt: _____
Why this triggered me: _____

Date: _____ Time: _____ Place: _____
What triggered me? _____
Knee-jerk reaction: _____
Physical sensation: _____
I thought: _____
I felt: _____
Why this triggered me: _____

Date: _____ Time: _____ Place: _____
What triggered me? _____
Knee-jerk reaction: _____
Physical sensation: _____
I thought: _____
I felt: _____
Why this triggered me: _____

Date: _____ Time: _____ Place: _____
What triggered me? _____
Knee-jerk reaction: _____
Physical sensation: _____
I thought: _____
I felt: _____
Why this triggered me: _____

Date: _____ Time: _____ Place: _____
What triggered me? _____
Knee-jerk reaction: _____
Physical sensation: _____
I thought: _____
I felt: _____
Why this triggered me: _____

Date: _____ Time: _____ Place: _____
What triggered me? _____
Knee-jerk reaction: _____
Physical sensation: _____
I thought: _____
I felt: _____
Why this triggered me: _____

Date: _____ Time: _____ Place: _____
What triggered me? _____
Knee-jerk reaction: _____
Physical sensation: _____
I thought: _____
I felt: _____
Why this triggered me: _____

Date: _____ Time: _____ Place: _____
What triggered me? _____
Knee-jerk reaction: _____
Physical sensation: _____
I thought: _____
I felt: _____
Why this triggered me: _____

Date: _____ Time: _____ Place: _____
What triggered me? _____
Knee-jerk reaction: _____
Physical sensation: _____
I thought: _____
I felt: _____
Why this triggered me: _____

Date: _____ Time: _____ Place: _____
What triggered me? _____
Knee-jerk reaction: _____
Physical sensation: _____
I thought: _____
I felt: _____
Why this triggered me: _____

Date: _____ Time: _____ Place: _____
What triggered me? _____
Knee-jerk reaction: _____
Physical sensation: _____
I thought: _____
I felt: _____
Why this triggered me: _____

Date: _____ Time: _____ Place: _____
What triggered me? _____
Knee-jerk reaction: _____
Physical sensation: _____
I thought: _____
I felt: _____
Why this triggered me: _____

Date: _____ Time: _____ Place: _____
What triggered me? _____
Knee-jerk reaction: _____
Physical sensation: _____
I thought: _____
I felt: _____
Why this triggered me: _____

Date: _____ Time: _____ Place: _____
What triggered me? _____
Knee-jerk reaction: _____
Physical sensation: _____
I thought: _____
I felt: _____
Why this triggered me: _____

Date: _____ Time: _____ Place: _____
What triggered me? _____
Knee-jerk reaction: _____
Physical sensation: _____
I thought: _____
I felt: _____
Why this triggered me: _____

Date: _____ Time: _____ Place: _____
What triggered me? _____
Knee-jerk reaction: _____
Physical sensation: _____
I thought: _____
I felt: _____
Why this triggered me: _____

Date: _____ Time: _____ Place: _____
What triggered me? _____
Knee-jerk reaction: _____
Physical sensation: _____
I thought: _____
I felt: _____
Why this triggered me: _____

Date: _____ Time: _____ Place: _____
What triggered me? _____
Knee-jerk reaction: _____
Physical sensation: _____
I thought: _____
I felt: _____
Why this triggered me: _____

Date: _____ Time: _____ Place: _____
What triggered me? _____
Knee-jerk reaction: _____
Physical sensation: _____
I thought: _____
I felt: _____
Why this triggered me: _____

Date: _____ Time: _____ Place: _____
What triggered me? _____
Knee-jerk reaction: _____
Physical sensation: _____
I thought: _____
I felt: _____
Why this triggered me: _____

Date: _____ Time: _____ Place: _____
What triggered me? _____
Knee-jerk reaction: _____
Physical sensation: _____
I thought: _____
I felt: _____
Why this triggered me: _____

Date: _____ Time: _____ Place: _____
What triggered me? _____
Knee-jerk reaction: _____
Physical sensation: _____
I thought: _____
I felt: _____
Why this triggered me: _____

Date: _____ Time: _____ Place: _____
What triggered me? _____
Knee-jerk reaction: _____
Physical sensation: _____
I thought: _____
I felt: _____
Why this triggered me: _____

Date: _____ Time: _____ Place: _____
What triggered me? _____
Knee-jerk reaction: _____
Physical sensation: _____
I thought: _____
I felt: _____
Why this triggered me: _____

More From Imaginate Publishing

FOR THE BOLD & BRAVE

12 Month Dated Agenda With Weekly AA Slogans & Sobriety Tracker
The Brave Guide: A Workbook & Guide For Those Brave Enough To Quit!
90 Meetings In 90 Days Guided AA Meeting Journal & Tracker
An AA's Little Handbook Of Hope Prayers Inspiration & Laughs
Get That Funky Monkey Off My Back! (Sweary Smoker's Trigger Tracker)
Five Minute Guided Trigger Tracker & Behavior Checker
Diary Of An Addict: 5 Minute Guided Trigger Tracker With Daily Journal
AA Powerful 12 Step Workbook With Trigger Tracker & Selfcare Check-Ins
AA 12 Step Workbook: Twelve Steps Journal To Sobriety
Stepping Through The First 90 Days: 12 Step Journal With Steps 10 - 12
The Power Of Powerlessness: Powerful AA Step 1 Workbook & Journal
Fourth Step Workbook: AA Journal For Alcohol Recovery
Making Our 4-Column Grudge List: A 4th Step Inventory Workbook
Into Action: The Art Of Swapping Character Defects For Character Assets
Journaling Through The Next Six Months: 10th Step Journal
10th Step Inventory Journal: Step 10 Nightly Inventory
My 10th Step Inventory Journal - For Steps 10, 11, & 12

IN A BELIEVER'S TOOLBOX

A Believer's Walk With Jesus: Chronological Gospel Reading Plan & Journal
A Believer's Walk In Wisdom: 12 Flexible Bible Reading Plans & Journal
Journey Through The Bible: Chronological Bible Reading Plan & Journal
4-Month Bible Study Planner & Journal With Weekly Bible Verse
Inductive Bible Study Journal With 90 Guided Entries
Bible Study Journal: Drawing Closer To God (Soap Bible Study Prompts)
200 Page Notebook With Inspirational Quotes From The Bible
Gratitude Journal With Inspirational Quotes From The Bible
Undated Planner & Bible Study Journal: Making Time For God: 1 Year
Planner & Bible Study Journal (1 Year Dated - Blue or Orange)

JOURNALS FROM IMAGINATE

Making Love To My Demons: Shadow Work Guided Journal & Workbook
One Line A Day 5 Year Journal: The Story Of Me
From Russell Conwell's Acres Of Diamonds: A Success Journal
Cocktail Recipe Journal: Blank Cocktail & Mixed Drink Recipe Book
My Badass Cocktails: Blank Cocktail Recipe Book
My Badass Recipes: Blank Recipe Notebook Journal
100 Family Recipes Blank Recipe Journal
101 Recipes: Blank Recipe Notebook

Planners & Notebooks From Imaginate

SUCCESS IS PLANNED – PERSONAL PLANNERS

The Sophisticated Financial Budget Planner: Monthly, Weekly, Daily
Undated Sunflowers & Butterflies Monthly & Weekly Planner
Undated Planner & Bible Study Journal: Making Time For God (12 months)
18 Month Midyear Academic Planner For April – September
12 Month Midyear Academic Planner For July – June
Planner & Bible Study Journal (1 Year Dated - Blue or Orange)
12 Month Dated Agenda With Weekly AA Slogans & Sobriety Tracker
12 Month Personal Planner: Monthly, Weekly & Daily - Pretty Purple Floral
12 Month Personal Planner: Monthly, Weekly & Daily
Two Year Monthly & Weekly Planner With Quotes
Two Year Monthly Planner With Quotes
Five Year Monthly Planner: 60 Month Agenda To Smash Your Goals

BEAUTIFULLY WATERMARKED DESIGNER NOTEBOOKS

Sunflowers & Butterflies: 120 Beautifully Watermarked Pages.
Silly Christmas Reindeer - 200 Pages College-Ruled or Wide-Ruled
Delightful Christmas Gnome - 200 Pages College-Ruled or Wide-Ruled
Magical Christmas Train - 200 Pages College-Ruled or Wide-Ruled
Shiny Christmas Tree - 200 Pages College-Ruled or Wide-Ruled
Cute Christmas Snowman - 200 Pages College-Ruled or Wide-Ruled
Falling Snow Flakes - 200 Pages College-Ruled or Wide-Ruled

VISIT THE BOLD & BRAVE
www.addictionrecoverybooks.com

VISIT IMAGINATE PUBLISHING
www.imaginateonline.com

Printed in Great Britain
by Amazon